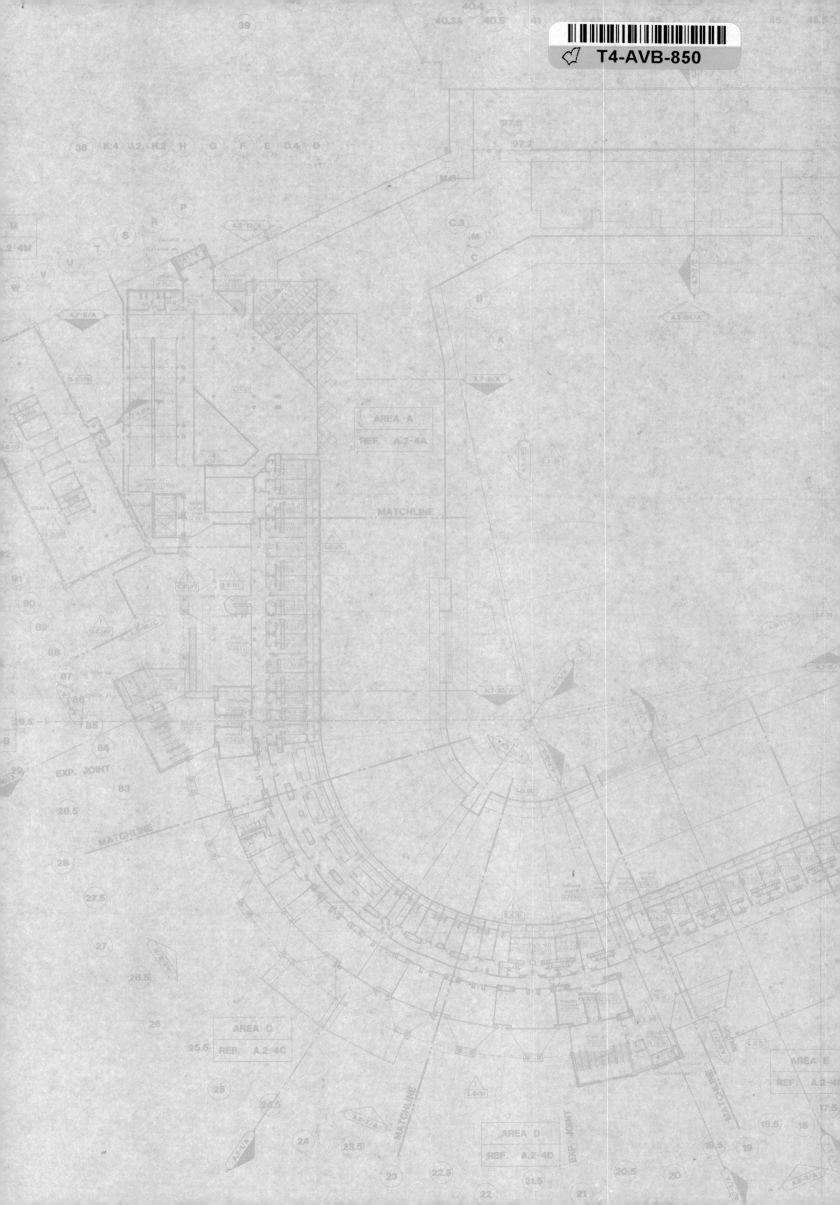

Gateway:

Book One:

Blueprint Of

Jacobs Field

The Future

By
Edward J. Walsh

Gateway:

Book One:

Blueprint Of

Jacobs Field

The Future

By
Edward J. Walsh

Published By
**Gateway Press
Incorporated**

Copyright 1994

Publisher
John A. Hocevar

Editor-in-Chief
Susan M. Tedrick

Editor
Rory O'Connor

Design and Art Direction
Benjamin J. Kotowski

Library of Congress
Catalog Card Number
94-75823

ISBN 0-934837-62-7

Printed by
S.P. Mount & Company
Cleveland, Ohio

"Make no little plans,
they have no magic to stir
men's blood."

– Daniel Burnham
1846—1912

Burnham was the architect
of Cleveland's Group Plan for The Mall,
which today includes
the Cuyahoga County Courthouse,
Public Hall and Auditorium,
the Federal Building,
Cleveland City Hall,
the Cleveland Public Library,
the Federal Reserve Bank Building
and the Board of Education
Administration Building.

More Than Just a Stadium

In the spring of 1990, a slogan was developed
to help convince the public of Cuyahoga
County that it should support a tax subsidy
for a new ballpark. The slogan was
"Gateway—More Than Just a Stadium."

The Gateway project is not only a first-class ballpark for the Cleveland Indians; it is also a first-class arena for the Cleveland Cavaliers, the Lumberjacks, the Thunderbolts, and a variety of world-class entertainment. Gateway is also parking, an RTA accessway, and public spaces to be enjoyed by people throughout Northeast Ohio year round.

Just the events that take place here make these buildings important, but they are also significant architectural prizes for Greater Cleveland. Great attention was paid to the urban aesthetics so that these buildings would not only be "fan friendly", but objects of pride for Greater Clevelanders. The buildings define the southern boundary of downtown Cleveland.

The Gateway project is more than just a stadium in that it provides a significant amount of work for people in Cleveland, Cuyahoga County, and the surrounding communities. More than 4,000 people actually worked on the site during the two-and-a-half year construction period. Nearly five times that number worked in area factories, mills, and shops creating and fabricating the materials that make up the Gateway complex. The vast majority of the $425 million spent on this project as a whole was recycled right back into the community.

But Gateway is also more than just a stadium because of what it will do for the downtown area in the long run. As Mayor Michael White said, "Gateway is important because it is a catalyst for redeveloping a portion of our downtown that had been virtually abandoned." The Historic Gateway Neighborhood, indeed the entire southern edge of downtown, has been revitalized as more than five million fans each year come to enjoy themselves at the Gateway sports and entertainment center. In the future, more people will live in the Historic Gateway Neighborhood, and commercial development will accompany them.

Finally, Gateway is more than just a stadium because of the lift that this project gave to the spirit of Greater Clevelanders. Building a ballpark and an arena is not, alone, the permanent cure for our urban problems. The teamwork, spirit of cooperation, and partnership which led to its becoming a reality put us on a firm path towards proving that Cleveland is a city where ethnic and racial diversity work successfully to convert the city's vision into reality.

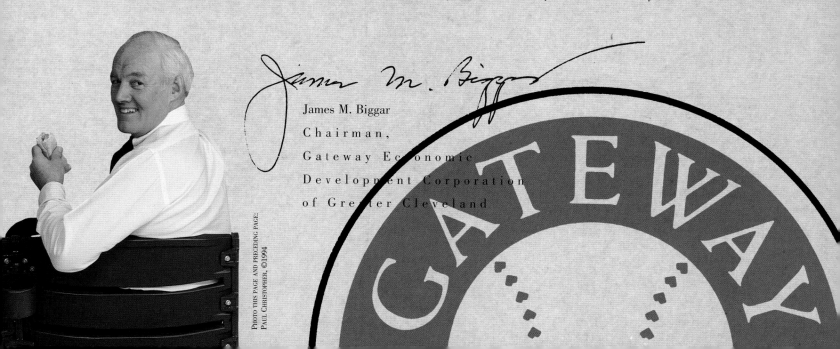

James M. Biggar
Chairman,
Gateway Economic
Development Corporation
of Greater Cleveland

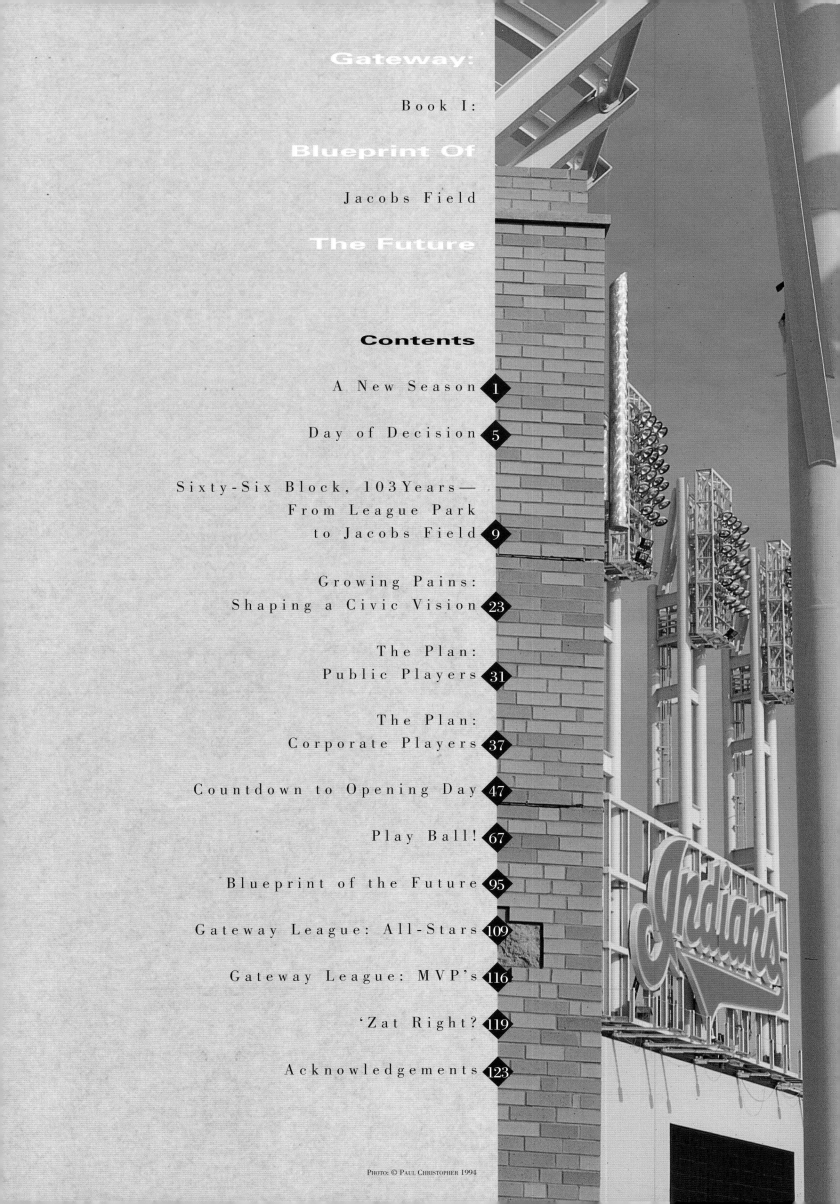

Gateway:

Book I:

Blueprint Of

Jacobs Field

The Future

Contents

PHOTO: © PAUL CHRISTOPHER 1994

A New Season

Like a genie uncorked from a bottle,

Gateway began as nothing more than

an amorphous civic vision that floated

about freely, slowly taking shape in

the minds of farsighted civic, business,

and political leaders.

PHOTO: © JENNIE JONES 1993

But these men and women were anything but idle dreamers. They were both practical and altruistic, both doers and visionaries. They understood that there were fundamental reasons why Cleveland, a comeback city of the 1980s, needed and deserved a modern, first-class professional sports and entertainment complex.

Even as the City of Cleveland had set about remaking and reenergizing itself in the mid-1980s, the future of the Indians in Cleveland was questionable at best. Both the Commissioner of Baseball, Peter Ueberroth, and the President of the American League, Dr. Bobby Brown, warned that the future of the Indians, one of only four original American League franchises still in its hometown, was in jeopardy.

So the need for Gateway became even more urgent. A world-class baseball park in a world-class facility would prove beyond any doubt that Cleveland, its fans, and its people were committed to the team and to the game.

The people who dreamed this dream did not stop there. They envisioned Gateway as the future home not only of professional baseball but of other professional sports. Didn't it make sense to build an arena that would become the permanent home of the Cleveland Cavaliers of the National Basketball Association? A facility that, like the Cleveland Arena that once had stood on Euclid Avenue at East 36th Street, could also become a home for hockey, concerts, and other events? You bet it made sense, the dreamers said.

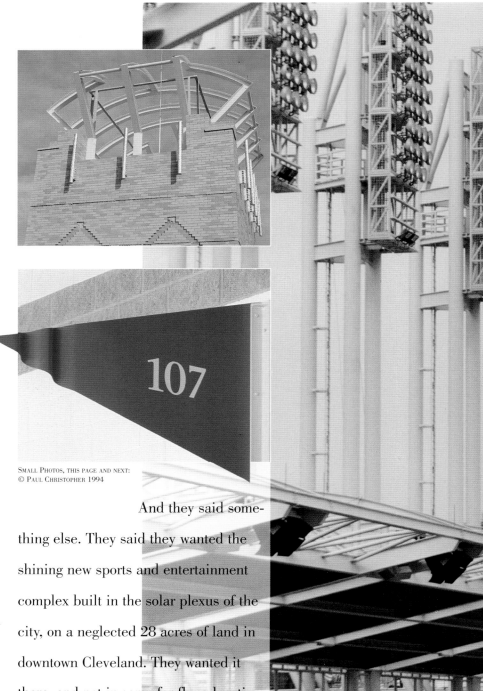

SMALL PHOTOS, THIS PAGE AND NEXT:
© PAUL CHRISTOPHER 1994

And they said something else. They said they wanted the shining new sports and entertainment complex built in the solar plexus of the city, on a neglected 28 acres of land in downtown Cleveland. They wanted it there, and not in some far-flung location, for some very down-to-earth reasons. The site would be one that the fans who lived and breathed and laughed and cried with the Indians and the Cavaliers could get to easily. The complex would be a glittering new jewel in that southern portion of downtown that had been passed over in Cleveland's renaissance. Its luster would rub off on the neglected neighborhood, revitalizing the area with hotels, office buildings, shops, and jobs.

PHOTOS, ABOVE: © SKYVIEW PHOTOGRAPHY 1994

The dream then became a vision, and it came to be called "Gateway".

Now Gateway is everything those visionaries imagined it would be: the showpiece of downtown Cleveland.

Jacobs Field, the $170 million open-air ballpark, seats 42,500 people, and is the home of the Cleveland Indians. The $124 million, 21,000-seat Arena is the permanent home of the Cleveland Cavaliers.

With its distinctive architecture, festival plaza, and specially commissioned artwork, the complex is truly a Gateway to downtown and, moreover, to the future of Cleveland and Northeast Ohio.

The sun rose

warm and red

over the lakefront

on May 8, 1990.

It was to be a

decisive day

in Cleveland's

history.

The people of
Cleveland and Cuyahoga County were
about to vote on a 15-year tax on the
wholesale cost of cigarettes, beer, and
wine, and a wholesale and retail tax on
liquor sold in state stores.

This excise tax was
to pay for approximately 50 percent of
an ambitious proposal for a $425 million
sports complex called Gateway. The
complex would include an open-air ballpark and an arena for basketball, hockey
and other indoor sports, and special
events. Just as important, said Gateway
proponents, Gateway would be the catalyst for the development of the surrounding neighborhood, a weary pocket
of downtown Cleveland known as the
Central Market site, now only bedrag-
gled streets and weather-worn buildings.

The tax had been a
topic of hot debate throughout the city
and county for weeks. Married couples
debated it, office workers argued it, radio
talk show hosts pontificated about it.

T he excise tax vote would shape
the future for Cleveland,
its baseball team, and for
Thomas V. Chema, who had
devised the financial package
that would make the Gateway
project possible.

PHOTO: © PAUL CHRISTOPHER 1994 (RIGHT)

Supporters of the tax argued that without it, Gateway could not be built. If it were not built, the city very well might lose the Cleveland Indians, and also lose a golden opportunity to develop the southern extremity of downtown. Opponents retorted that this tax — or any new tax to build Gateway, for that matter — penalized the poor. Why should the public subsidize a private, for-profit enterprise like the Indians? went the argument. A smart bookie would have made the odds even on the tax passing.

Of all the people who argued the merits of the tax, at least one person had bet his reputation, perhaps even his career, on its passage. This was Thomas V. Chema, a partner with the Cleveland law firm of Arter & Hadden and former chairman of the Public Utilities Commission of Ohio.

A year earlier, Chema had been asked by then-Governor Richard F. Celeste to jump start the stalled Gateway project, which was mired in financial and public relations difficulties. Chema had responded positively, and now the excise tax, a critical part of the financial package Chema helped devise, was about to face the test of the ballot box.

"At the time of the vote, there was no Gateway organization as such," Chema says. "We were just a loose campaign team, an ad hoc entity."

Campaign headquarters was on the street level of the BP America Building, on Public Square. Reports made it clear that voting was heavy. When the polls finally closed at 7:30 p.m., Chema invited several people from the campaign committee to join him for dinner at Gershwin's, a restaurant in the BP building.

The Indians, who were given their name in 1915, are the only team in major league baseball to be named in honor of an individual — Louis "Chief" Sockalexis, a Penobscot Indian and gifted athlete who played for the Cleveland Spiders in the 1890s. The team had a number of other names, including the Blues or Bluebirds (1900), the Broncos (1902), the Naps -- after popular player-manager Napoleon Lajoie -- (1903), and the Molly Maguires (1912).

PHOTO: BASEBALL HALL OF FAME AND MUSEUM (FACING PAGE)

There were some who thought Chema had perhaps pushed too hard to get the levy on the May ballot, that it would have been more prudent to wait. Chema, though, was convinced that a "blitzkrieg" was absolutely crucial to get the stalled Gateway project off dead center.

Now, however, there was nothing to do but return to campaign headquarters, talk to pollsters, and watch the returns on TV. The vote was just too close to call.

That night Tom Chema watched the 11 o'clock news

and

waited.

Louis "Chief" Sockalexis

Sixty-Six Blocks,

103 Years—

From League Park

to Jacobs Field

Soon after the game was invented, baseball was played in Cleveland. As early as 1857, only 12 years after the first game was played in Hoboken, New Jersey, under the modern rules devised by Alexander Cartwright, some of Cleveland's genteel citizens were protesting "ball playing" on Public Square.

Ball playing on Cleveland's Public square was expressly forbidden by city ordinance until the law was changed in 1856 to prohibit "defacing" the park . The new law, posted on the fence surrounding the square, can be seen in the photo at left.

Legend has it that shortly after the new ordinance was posted, the town marshal was summoned to put a stop to a baseball game in progress. The sympathetic official, upon reading the new ordinance, declared that he had no authority to act. By 1859, when this photo was taken, a baseball diamond had clearly been worn into the grass, with home plate, pitchers mound, and baselines all clearly visible.

PHOTO: THE OHIO HISTORICAL SOCIETY

For more than a decade after Municipal Stadium was completed in 1932, the Indians kept playing at League Park, popular because of what one sportswriter called its "intimate dimensions." The team didn't play at the Stadium full time until 1947.

In 1865, the Forest Citys, an organized Cleveland amateur baseball team, played its first game against the Penfields of Oberlin. Even with the home-field advantage, the Forest Citys suffered a 67 to 28 loss.

Four years later the Forest Citys hired three professional players, and played its first pro game against the nation's first professional team, the Cincinnati Red Stockings, on June 2, 1869. Cleveland lost, 25 to 6.

Over the next few years, Cleveland fielded teams in some of the emerging baseball associations, and, for a time, was without any ballclub.

Then, in 1879, a new Forest City team joined the National League, which had been organized in 1876. On June 12, 1880, the club was on the losing end of professional baseball's first perfect game, pitched by John Lee Richmond of the Worcester, Massachusetts, ball club.

In 1885, the Forest Citys discreetly withdrew from the National League. But another Cleveland team joined the National League in 1889. It had played for two seasons in the American Association, affectionately known as the "beer and whiskey league" because its rules did not forbid quaffing alcohol.

Owners Frank DeHaas Robison and George W. Howe had built a ballpark for their club at Payne Avenue and East 39th Street in 1887, so the "Spiders," as the new National League entry was known, already had a home field.

The Spiders were no pushovers, fielding a team that featured manager Pat Tebeau, catcher Charles Zimmer, and legendary pitcher Denton True "Cy" Young.

No, it's not short for "Cyril." Denton True Young threw so hard that local sportswriters, ever creative with nicknames, dubbed him "Cyclone," which soon was shortened to "Cy." Young, for whom major league baseball's top pitching award is named, was purchased by the Cleveland Spiders from a Canton team for $250 in 1890.

PHOTO: CLEVELAND STATE UNIVERSITY

On May 1, 1891, Young pitched the opening game at National League Park, the club's brand new field. Located at East 66th Street and Lexington Avenue, just a few steps from the trolley line owned by Robison, the brick structure held more than 9,000 fans who watched the Spiders beat the Cincinnati Redlegs, 12 to 3.

When League Park opened in 1891:

☛ Women (called "ladies" in those dark old days) were admitted free to the grandstand every day except Saturdays and holidays.

☛ "Never on Sunday" was the National League rule. But that was circumvented - fans were admitted "free" - but only with the purchase of a scorecard!

PHOTO: WESTERN RESERVE HISTORICAL SOCIETY

Robison more than likely watched the game from the comfort of a box in the wooden stands reserved for the team president.

At the end of the 1892 season, when Cleveland played in the National League, playoffs between the Boston Beaneaters and the Spiders were held at League Park. Needing a

An indignant Robison gutted his own team in 1898, sending his best players, including Cy Young, to a club he had purchased in St. Louis. In 1899 the Spiders were derisively known by fans as the "Misfits". They played most of their games on the road, finishing the season with a disastrous record of 20 victories and 134 defeats. The following

PANORAMA VIEW NEW AMERICAN LEAGUE B

name for the new playoffs, sportswriters called them the "World Series."

The fortunes of the Spiders peaked in 1895 and 1896, when they qualified to play a final series with the league-leading Baltimore Orioles by finishing in second place. They beat the Orioles in 1895 but lost to them in a four-game sweep the following year.

Things began to unravel for the Spiders in the next few years, and attendance plummeted.

year the National League cut its roster to eight teams, and Cleveland was among the four cities unceremoniously dumped.

The Spiders were no more, but Ban Johnson, founder of the American League, moved a minor league club from Grand Rapids, Michigan, to Cleveland. In 1901 the Cleveland Bluebirds, better known as the Blues, became a charter member of the new American League, and finished in seventh place.

The Blues were the true genesis of the Indians. Their owners, Cleveland coal merchant Charles W. Somers, his father, and clothing store owner John F. Kilfoyl, negotiated a lease agreement to remain at League Park. Somers was instrumental in keeping, not only the Cleveland franchise, but the fledgling American League

1909 League Park's wooden grandstand was replaced by double-decked stands for 27,000 fans. Individual box seats were available for the first time.

League Park was made for left-handed pull hitters, who only had to clear 290 feet down the right-field line for a home run. Right-handed hitters had to pull the ball 375

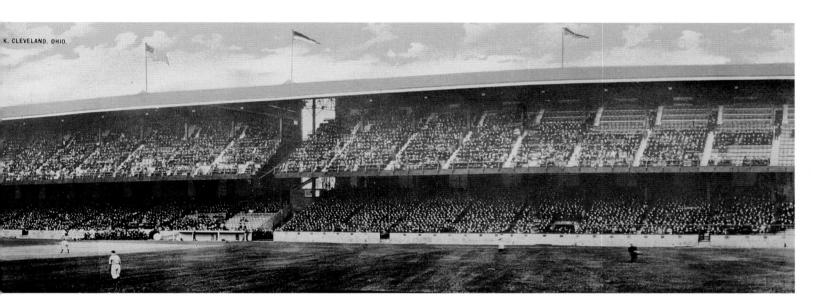

K, CLEVELAND, OHIO.

alive. He invested $1 million in the new league teams, including loaning Charley Comiskey the money he needed to build his new ballpark in Chicago.

In June of 1902 the new owners made a brilliant move, acquiring second baseman Napoleon Lajoie from the Philadelphia Athletics. Officially, the team name was the "Broncos", but in short order everybody in town called them the "Naps". Sparked by Lajoie's talent and popularity, the team played to overflow crowds. In

In 1909, League Park was transformed from a simple wooden structure (which was struck by lightning and burned in 1892) into a then ultra-modernistic facility with a double-deck steel grandstand.

Osborne Engineering, which designed both League Park and Jacobs Field, recently discovered that its designers had incorporated the old box office building into the the 1909 "new" ballpark design. Today, the box office, fashioned of brick and shaped like a house, and a small portion of the grandstand, still stand on the northwest corner of East 66th Street and Lexington Avenue.

Although player-manager Napoleon Lajoie

was so popular that during his 12 years in Cleveland

the team was referred to as the "Naps", the name

did not survive Lajoie's trade to St. Louis in 1915.

feet along the left field line to clear the fence. The distance to dead center was 420 feet. But the replacement of the old wooden fence with 20 feet of concrete and another 25 feet of chicken wire made the right field corner a difficult one — baseballs hit against the wall in right field caromed crazily.

Still in search of a name that would stick, the team was christened the "Molly Maguires" in 1912. Fans weren't buying this odd moniker either — the Molly Maguires were a 19th century secret society of Pennsylvania miners who engaged in terrorism for better working conditions. The club was still popularly known as the "Naps", and after a dismal 1914 season, in which they lost 102 games, the team underwent a major shakeup.

In 1915, Lajoie was traded and Charles Somers sold the team to Chicago businessman James C. "Sunny Jim" Dunn. The club again was renamed, this time as a result of a contest. The winning name was the Indians, in honor of Louis Francis "Chief" Sockalexis, a Penobscot Indian who played outfield for the Spiders from 1897 to 1899. Perhaps the biggest news of all was the purchase of Tristram "Tris" Speaker from Boston for a whopping $50,000.

In 1916, his first year with the team, Speaker won the league batting championship, hitting .386. Named player-manager in 1919, Speaker led the Indians to their first American League pennant in 1920. Dunn celebrated by renaming League Park "Dunn Field", and the Indians headed east to face the Brooklyn Trolley Dodgers in the 1920 World Series.

Guess who owns these records in Cleveland (hint: it's one person): *the highest single-season batting average (.408 in 1911), most hits in a season (233 in 1911), most triples in a season (26 in 1912), and the highest lifetime batting average (.375). None other than the legendary "Shoeless" Joe Jackson. After his time in Cleveland, Jackson joined the Chicago White Sox. As every fan knows, it was alleged that Joe was among a number of "Black Sox" players who caved in to gamblers and threw the 1919 World Series. It was the worst scandal in major league baseball history, and directly led to the creation of the Office of the Commissioner of Baseball. The first commissioner, Judge Kenesaw "Mountain" Landis, demanded absolute independence from team owners, then permanently banished the offending players.*

The Indians lost two of the first three games to the Dodgers before returning to League Park to win four straight games and the Series.

In 1927, the Dunn family sold the Indians to a local syndicate that included Newton D. Baker, who had been mayor of Cleveland and Secretary of War under President Woodrow Wilson; Baker's law partner, Joseph Hostetler; Charles and Alva Bradley, of the shipbuilding Bradley family; and Oris P. and Mantis J. Van Sweringen, the bachelor brothers who were building the $179 million Terminal Tower complex. The new owners renamed the club's home field "League Park".

By this time, city fathers had shown interest in building a stadium north of Lakeside Avenue. There, thousands of carloads of fill material were being dumped along the

A *spectacular moment in League Park's history: the day in 1929 when Yankee Babe Ruth hit his 500th home run over the right-field wall. The "Sultan of Swat" rewarded the kid who returned the ball, Jack Geiser, with a $20 bill, an autographed ball, and a seat in the Yankee dugout.*

PHOTO: WESTERN RESERVE HISTORICAL SOCIETY

Even the legendary Babe Ruth had never seen anything like Cleveland's gigantic Stadium. With individual seating for 78,189 people, it was the largest outdoor facility of its kind in the world when it opened in 1932. Ruth took one look at the field and declared, "The only way a man can play this outfield is on a horse!"

lakefront between East Ninth and West Third streets. William R. Hopkins, the city manager, had preliminary plans drawn up, and a citizens' committee devised more than 60 possible uses for a new stadium. These included everything from musical entertainment to business expositions and wrestling matches, as well as professional, college, and high school sports.

The public became enthusiastic about the project. In November of 1928 a bond issue for $2.5 million to construct a new stadium was approved by the city electorate.

Bulldozers arrived at the stadium site June 24, 1930. In little more than a year the massive stadium, measuring 800 feet in length, 720 feet in width, and 115 feet in

height, was completed. The formal dedication took place the evening of July 2, 1931, when a disappointing crowd of only 8,000 showed up for the ceremonies.

The city hoped to sign a lease with the Indians. Negotiations, however, moved slowly.

On July 31, 1932, the Indians played their first game in the cavernous new Stadium. In front of a record-breaking crowd of 80,184 fans, Mel Harder lost a 1-0 decision to Lefty Grove of the Philadelphia Athletics.

But Cleveland Municipal Stadium was not built along the comfortable lines of a pure baseball stadium. Its vast playing field, later cut down to size by the erection of a

The Cleveland Buckeyes were the best, and last, of Cleveland teams that played in the Negro leagues. Teams came and went, under such names as "Tate Stars," "Browns," "Elites," "Hornets," "Cubs," "Stars," "Giants," "Red Sox," and "Bears," and played at Hardware Field, Luna Bowl, Cubs Park, Hooper Field, and Tate Park. The Cleveland Cubs' claim to fame was that Leroy Satchel Paige, their featured pitcher in 1931, finished his career with the Cleveland Indians.

fence, proved troublesome not only to opposing hitters, but to the Indians lineup as well.

Baseball fans complained about the great size of the new Stadium. It was only 320 feet from home plate along the foul lines, but the field stretched 470 feet to the center field bleacher wall. No ball was ever hit into the Stadium's center-field bleachers.

Attendance in 1932 and '33 was disappointing. In 1934 the Indians returned to League Park for most of their home games, using Cleveland Stadium only on Sundays, holidays, and special occasions.

The team continued to split its home schedule between League Park and the Stadium for the next 12 years. Plenty of fans still remember when Yankee great Joe DiMaggio's hitting streak over 56 consecutive games was set on July 16, 1941, at League Park — a record that still stands — but ended the next day at Municipal Stadium.

League Park and Municipal Stadium hosted other Cleveland teams – from the Negro leagues. In 1945, the Buckeyes won the Negro World Series, and won the Negro National League pennant in 1947. Though drawing crowds of up to 10,000, they still lost money, and folded the following year. They unsuccessfully attempted a comeback in 1950, calling it quits after half a season, and the Negro League era in Cleveland came to a close.

After Jackie Robinson signed with the Yankees (National League), and Larry Doby joined the Indians (American League), within months of each other in 1947, the color barrier was effectively broken. Other Negro league players were soon snapped up by the Indians, including Luke Easter and Satchel Paige.

In 1946, the Indians were sold to promotional genius and baseball legend Bill Veeck. Convinced he could fill the Stadium, Veeck vacated League Park permanently. The Tribe played its last game there on September 21, 1946.

Veeck had big plans for the Stadium. In 1947, a fence was installed in the outfield, trimming 70 feet from the distance to dead center field. And Veeck began his legacy of promotions, which that year drew 1.5 million fans.

In 1948, a year of pennant fever, the Indians set a new attendance record of 2,620,627 paid fans. Led by shortstop manager Lou Boudreau, third baseman Ken Keltner and second baseman Joe Gordon, the Indians finished the season in a first-place tie with the Boston Red Sox. Defeating the Red Sox in a one-game playoff, 8-3, the Tribe faced the Boston Braves in the World Series. The Indians won the Series, four games to two. A crowd of 300,000 people welcomed the world champions home from their Series win in Boston.

The club won the pennant again in 1954, anchored by the "Big Four" pitching staff of Early Wynn, Bob Lemon, Mike Garcia and Bob Feller. Manager Al Lopez led the club to an all-time American League mark of 111 wins, but lost the World Series to the New York Giants in a four-game sweep.

The loss to the Giants seemed to sap the energy from the club. A series of misfortunes followed, which Indians fans blamed on everything from curses to incompetence. In 1957, promising young left-hander Herb Score was struck in the right eye by a line drive off the bat of Yankee Gil McDougald. Score recovered and returned to the Tribe in 1958, but never regained the form that enabled him to compile a 20-9 record in 1956.

Things got worse.

Frank Lane, named General Manager in 1958, traded

*H*all of Fame pitcher "Rapid" Robert Feller pitched three no-hitters in his career. The first was April 16, 1940, a 1-0 victory at Chicago. It remains baseball's only opening-day no-hitter.

Feller boasts at least nine Indians pitching records, including: ☞ most games won (266), ☞ most completed games (279), ☞ most innings pitched (3,828), ☞ most strike outs (2,581), and ☞ most shutouts (46)

immensely popular outfielder Rocky Colavito to Detroit for outfielder Harvey Kuenn in 1960. Disbelieving fans were stunned. Later in the season, Lane traded Indians manager Joe Gordon to Detroit for manager Jimmie Dykes. Nothing helped the faltering Tribe, and attendance plummeted.

Gabe Paul, hired to replace Lane in 1961, bought controlling interest in the team in 1962. He served as team president for nine years, moved to New York, and returned to Cleveland as president from 1978 through 1984.

During those years, ownership of the Tribe resembled a game of "hot potato": Paul, '62-'67; Vernon Stouffer, '67 – '72; Nick Mileti, '72 – '76; Alva T. "Ted" Bonda (controlling interest), '77 – '78; F. J. "Steve" O'Neill, '78. The O'Neill family retained control of the club through the

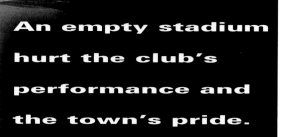

'86 season, when it was sold to Richard and David Jacobs, who finally returned stable ownership to the Indians.

Only three times did attendance for the Tribe hit the million mark between 1960 and 1980. And only once, in 1968, did they finish as high as third place. The Indians had fallen, to say the very least, on hard times.

But in spite of the problems, the team and the Stadium did provide memorable moments. Their only perfect game (as the "Indians") and the only one at the Stadium, kept fans breathless as Len Barker scored a 3-0 victory over Toronto on May 15, 1981.

The huge Stadium and the fans who filled it from time to time

still established attendance records, but the Cleveland Browns were often as not the main draw. After the 1970 merger between the NFL and AFL, ABC Television premiered Monday Night Football, featuring the Browns against the New York Jets, at the Stadium.

In its time, the Stadium had been the site of high school sports, college football, religious events, rock concerts and wrestling matches. During the years of Bill Veeck's ownership of the Tribe, new baseball attendance records had been set as a matter of course. But new ballparks were going up around the United States in the 1970s and '80s, and Cleveland Municipal Stadium was looking steadily the worse for wear.

In 1974, unable to pay for its upkeep, the city negotiated a 25-year lease on the stadium with Cleveland Browns majority owner Art Modell. Improvements were made, but baseball fans, other teams and their owners became increasingly dissatisfied with baseball played in a stadium never really designed for the game.

Talk was in the air that something new was needed.

Frank Robinson (opposite page) made his debut as the first black manager of a major league team on opening day, April 8, 1975. In his new role as player-manager for the Tribe, he scored a home run off Yankee pitcher Doc Medich his first time at bat.

Municipal Stadium holds other memories as well, like the stormy day in 1938 (right) when the lights had to be turned on to finish a game. And on October 10, 1948, the all-time attendance record for a single major league game was set when an incredible 86,288 fans crammed in to watch the Indians win the World Series.

PHOTO: ABOVE, CLEVELAND PUBLIC LIBRARY, © BETEMAN ARCHIVES. LEFT, CLEVELAND INDIANS

Growing Pains—
Shaping a Civic Vision

In 1983, rumors of a movement involving civic and business leaders who were going to propose a plan for a new domed stadium circulated throughout Cleveland.

Despite the millions of dollars invested in the Stadium by Art Modell's Stadium Corporation, there was a growing consensus in town that it no longer suited the needs of major league baseball.

In spite of years of lackluster home team performance, baseball remained Cleveland's favorite pastime, a vital (and largely untapped) economic force in the region.

PHOTO: DOME STADIUM CORPORATION

The Domed Stadium originally proposed for Cleveland was developed by Hellmuth, Obata, & Kassabaum, Inc. (HOK), who later designed the ballpark at Gateway.

Concerns about the future of baseball at the Stadium also deepened because of the death of F. J. O'Neill, principal owner of the team, in the summer of 1983. As a part of O'Neill's family trust, the club eventually would be sold. The worry was that it would be sold to an out-of-town buyer who would remove the team to another city.

The rumors about a planned domed stadium were more than idle gossip. In the clubs and corridors where Cleveland's business leadership gathered, there indeed was conversation about the need for a new stadium. At that point, however, talk centered on a combined-use facility for baseball and football. What was finally proposed were plans for a retractable dome — the first in the U.S. — seating 50,000 for baseball and 72,000 for football.

Growing Pains–Shaping A Civic Vision **24**
Gateway: Blueprint Of The Future

By February of 1984, Cuyahoga County Commissioners had determined they wanted the domed stadium issue on the May ballot, in the form of a 0.9 mill property tax. Vincent C. Campanella, the County Commission President, spearheaded the effort. The proposed cost of the dome was $150 million. If the issue was approved, county residents would pay for the dome with property taxes over 25 years. Proponents and opponents of the property tax squared off in a heated campaign.

The morning of May 8, the day Cuyahoga County voters went to the polls, was rain-swept and chilly. The temperature went no higher than the mid-50s. "V, The Final Battle" was on television that evening, as were Democratic primary election returns showing U.S. Senator Gary Hart with a slight lead over Walter Mondale in Ohio and Indiana.

After the defeat of the County Commissioners' property tax levy for a new domed stadium, grass roots supporters formed the Dome Boosters and began to canvass the county and hold special events to build public awareness and support for the project.

Early returns indicated that the dome issue was going to be defeated decisively. When the official results were finally in, the property tax and the dome had lost by a margin of two-to-one.

The loss at the polls was a severe setback to dome proponents, but it fell short of being fatal. Governor Celeste, for one, put the situation into political perspective. "I can't really call it a defeat for the dome," he told the media. He said that it was "more a defeat for the property tax issue."

Community leaders again considered the merits of a new downtown sports facility. They didn't flinch, again recommending that a new domed stadium be built for professional football and baseball, but this time with one-third public and two-thirds private financing.

In June of 1985, a new, not-for-profit corporation was formed. With the election of 33 permanent trustees, what had been a committee officially became The Greater Cleveland Domed Stadium Corporation. Allen C. Holmes, former managing partner of the law firm Jones, Day, Reavis & Pogue, was named chairman and president. Initial funding came from a $100,000 start-up grant from the State of Ohio. The grant was quickly matched by local businesses and foundations.

There were still many questions to be answered. Just what kind of a facility the Domed Stadium Corporation would recommend was not certain. Whether the public, whose support was still needed to build a dome, would look favorably on the project also was uncertain. But there was no question about the new stadium's site: the Central Market.

The city had spurred the initial development of this area in 1826, when it purchased land to create the Erie Street Cemetery. In the mid-19th century, City Council approved a site nearby for a public market, later called Central Market, at the intersection of Ontario and Broadway. The market gave rise to a large concentration of food storage, wholesale, and distribution businesses in the area, including a major competitor, the Sheriff Street Market. During the two 20th-century boom eras in downtown Cleveland — the 1920s and the 1980s — progress leapfrogged over this southern gateway to the city. Empty warehouses and parking lots were everywhere. Yet, to the astute eye of Albert B. Ratner, Gateway

activist and president and CEO of Forest City Enterprises, Inc., the land was a phenomenal bargain at slightly less than $1 million an acre. "It wasn't the best location for a stadium," recalls Ratner, "it was the only location."

In September of 1985, the City of Cleveland presented the Domed Stadium Corporation with its first building block: a parking lot at East 9th Street and Eagle Avenue. Soon after, the State of Ohio awarded the Domed Stadium Corporation a

Richard F.Celeste, at that time governor of Ohio, and George V. Voinovich, then mayor of Cleveland, confer at a Domed Stadium press conference.

$2 million grant for land acquisition, and loaned another $4 million to the Corporation itself. Local banks loaned $18 million to buttress acquisition efforts. Before the year was out, the Corporation purchased its first parcel of privately-owned land on the Central Market site.

There was cause for a sense of urgency on the part of dome proponents. In April of 1986, baseball commissioner Peter Ueberroth said the status of the Indians in Cleveland was "precarious." His dire statement, coupled with news that the Indians had debts of well over $11 million, fueled speculation that the Tribe was destined to be sold to out-of-town investors.

While the Domed Stadium Corporation focused on its tasks, speculation about a new buyer for the Indians continued. David LeFevre, a New York lawyer and grandson of Cleveland industrialist Cyrus Eaton, had made a serious bid for the team in 1984, but was soon considered out of the running. Rumors surfaced that New York real estate mogul Donald Trump was interested. Youngstown-based mall developer Edward J. DeBartolo was said to be a contender at one point. A Cleveland group, rumored to include Allen Holmes, was a fourth. More names bandied-about were those of Clevelanders Jeffrey Friedman, president of Associated Estates, Inc., and Milton Maltz, chairman of Malrite Communications Group, Inc. In July 1986, the news broke. Richard E. and David H. Jacobs, of Jacobs, Visconsi &

Jacobs Company (JVJ), a shopping mall development company headquartered in the Cleveland suburb of Westlake, were buying the Indians. With 39 regional malls in 14 states, JVJ was the fourth largest owner and manager of malls in the U.S. The Jacobs brothers, it was reported, intended to buy a 59

As early as the 1920s the Central Market area was in decline. In 1949, when the Market was destroyed by fire, 200 stalls moved across the street to the old Sheriff Street Market, closed since 1936. By 1981 fewer than 40 stalls remained, and the area continued to deteriorate.

percent share of the Indians from the O'Neill family trust, and then offered to buy out the remaining shareholders.

The arrival of the Jacobs brothers on the baseball scene was positive news, but the Corporation still faced some difficult obstacles. While the Ohio General Assembly had approved legislation that enabled Cuyahoga County to collect an excise tax to help finance the public portion of the dome's construction, the public would have to agree to pay such a tax. Convincing the public to tax themselves would not be an easy feat.

To further complicate matters, the Corporation would now have to negotiate lease terms with new — and unknown — Indians ownership. To top it off, they would have to work out terms with the Browns.

By the first months of 1987, hard realities had the Corporation reconsidering their funding options. "It became clear that it was going to take a lot more money than the private sector could raise," says Frank E. Mosier. As head of the Corporation's facilities committee, Mosier had visited new stadium facilities in the U. S. and Canada.

Photo: Western Reserve Historical Society

Questions also arose about the hazards faced by teams who played on the artificial surfaces required under a dome. Various options, including a canvas-topped dome, were considered, but thought to be too risky an investment. The price tag for a roofed, dual-purpose facility was too costly.

A charter change was adopted so that alternatives to dome designs could be considered, and the name was changed to the "New Stadium Corporation." Although there was more uncertainty than ever about exactly what would be built on the site, the demolition of the 28 acres began in earnest.

By the spring of 1988, all of the land necessary for construction of a new stadium was under the control of the Corporation, which had worked closely with Cleveland City Council and its powerful president, George L. Forbes. Holmes stepped aside as the Corporation's chairman and president, but only after meeting with Frank Mosier to make certain the BP America executive would take his place. What was to be built on the Central Market site and how it was to be financed were questions that remained unanswered. The thorny financial issues led finally, in Mosier's words, "to a stalemate."

In late spring of 1989, a new figure entered the picture, one who would face the challenge of breaking the deadlock and moving the project forward.

Tom Chema had recently finished his term as chairman of the Public Utilities Commission of Ohio under Governor Celeste. In May of 1989, Chema was invited to meet with Celeste at the Lausche State Office Building in downtown Cleveland. They would be joined by County Commissioner Mary Boyle, Celeste's principal aide in Northeast Ohio, Helen Williams, and several other aides and confidants of the governor.

The purpose of the meeting was straightforward. In the waning days of his administration, unable by law to run for another term, Celeste wanted the group to suggest what might be done to help Cleveland — the Governor's hometown — before he left office. Fears were expressed that the Indians still were in danger of being lost to another city. There was a consensus among the group that a last-ditch effort should be made to save the Indians. That meant somehow breaking the deadlock that now impeded progress on plans for the new stadium.

A month later Chema was invited to dine with the Governor at a downtown Cleveland restaurant. Some of the same people were again in attendance, including Mary Boyle and Helen Williams. That evening Chema was asked to serve as the Governor's stadium trouble-shooter to put together the financing package and convince the public and private sectors that their support of a new ballpark was in the best interest of the city and county.

Tom Chema suddenly had a very big job on his hands. He said "yes" to the project that came to be known as "Gateway."

The various parties trying to negotiate plans for a new stadium, meanwhile, discussed endless possibilities. In July, Indians owner Dick Jacobs, together with James Biggar, chairman of Cleveland Tomorrow, an economic development consortium, and Richard Shatten, Cleveland Tomorrow's then-executive

Legislation permitting a popular vote on an excise tax to finance the proposed stadium was signed into law at the Central Market site by Governor Celeste.

director, met with Cuyahoga County Commissioners Virgil E. Brown and Timothy F. Hagan to discuss proposals.

By August of 1989 there was no longer any doubt where the Jacobses stood on the issue of a new stadium. They had publicly expressed their desire for a new ballpark for the Indians at the Central Market site, and the Cleveland Browns were no longer part of the Gateway equation.

The Central Market area was, by the 1980s, largely vacant land or vacant buildings. This, and its strategic location near freeways, mass transit, and the heart of downtown, made it a choice location for the proposed dome, and later for Gateway. Ironically, when the Central Market was proposed in 1856, vendors protested the site as too far "uptown."

Within six months after taking on the Gateway project, Chema had developed and delivered a preliminary version of a revised stadium plan. It included an open-air ballpark and an indoor arena. The baseball stadium was for the Cleveland Indians; the arena, for, among others, the Cleveland Cavaliers.

With the Browns bowing out of the

picture, the Cavs suddenly played a major role in the project. The Cavs had played at the Richfield Coliseum, far from downtown Cleveland, since 1974. Now there was the possibility that the team, which played its first seasons in the NBA at the venerable Cleveland Arena at Euclid Avenue and East 40th Street, could be enticed to return to its hometown. Their return also would mean, recalls Cleveland City Councilwoman Helen Smith, that "Cleveland would benefit from a new revenue stream with the return of professional basketball to downtown Cleveland."

The blueprint that Chema laid out held a tantalizing benefit — the development of the area surrounding Gateway — that would become the capstone for the comeback of downtown Cleveland.

The Plan —
Public Players

The key to building Gateway was, in Tom Chema's opinion, nothing more or less than the excise tax. But in order to make the project viable, Chema felt the tax should be broader than first proposed.

After meeting with scores of officials, Chema developed the financing plan. The public would be asked to pay for half of the project by approving the excise tax. The remaining half was to be covered by the sale of bonds, retired by revenues from rentals of suites and club seats in both facilities.

The tax campaign committee, as Chema points out, was a volunteer-driven ad hoc group that relied on the efforts of politically skilled civic leaders such as committee chair Oliver "Pudge" Henkel and campaign manager Dennis Roche to provide the muscle.

But the support of the most influential elected officials also was essential, and Chema persistently solicited their help.

Two of the staunchest supporters were newly-elected Cleveland Mayor Michael R. White and County Commissioner Tim Hagan.

Chema had met with White twice before the new mayor took office. The first time was several months before the election, for an early breakfast in a coffee shop at the Cleveland Clinic. The second time was at the law firm of Hahn, Loeser & Parks, where the mayor-elect had set up a transitional office prior to moving into city hall.

White's foremost concern was that Gateway would bring major economic benefits to Cleveland. A new ballpark in and of itself did not, in White's opinion, hold much promise as a catalyst for generating development and jobs.

PHOTO: © RODNEY L. BROWN

*C*leveland's legendary Mayor Tom Johnson (facing page, about 1900, tossing a ceremonial baseball), demonstrated how responsible government investment could benefit the city's working people, creating public parks and establishing a municipal transit system.

In that great tradition, Mayor Michael R. White (right), and Cuyahoga County Commissioner Tim Hagan (above right), supported Gateway, convinced it would bring economic benefits to the people of Cleveland.

But combining it with a downtown arena was a totally different story, one that the new mayor listened to attentively. Presenting his case with the skills he acquired as an attorney, Chema convinced White that Gateway would indeed

From passing ordinances that facilitated construction to approving bond sales, Cleveland City Council and its president, Jay Westbrook (left), worked closely with Gateway, forging an alliance that has become the hallmark of the project.

PHOTO: STEVE ZORC

add economic luster to downtown Cleveland. It offered the opportunity for the physical renewal of downtown for investment, jobs, and participation by minority and female businesses. Some $20 million would be set aside for the purchase of adjacent land to spur revitalization.

Convinced of the need for the project, Mayor White "jumped in with both feet," recalls Chema.

It was a leap of political faith the mayor would not regret. And the benefits are exactly those he had hoped to see. "The exciting part of Gateway for me," says the mayor today, "is not the ballpark and the arena. The exciting part is how we can use them to rebuild the southwest quadrant of downtown Cleveland."

At almost the same moment that Mayor White committed

himself to Gateway, so too did County Commissioner Tim Hagan. His joining the mayor on the politically controversial issue was a one-two punch on the project's behalf.

Convinced that Gateway would indeed be a boon to the city, both White and Hagan publicly and vigorously supported the excise tax. Prior to election day, they walked the streets of downtown Cleveland pumping hands and campaigning for its passage. This was dangerous stuff in the minds of many more timid elected officials who had not forgotten the political smash-ups caused by the 1984 vote on public financing of a new stadium, when voters overwhelmingly rejected the property tax proposal for a domed stadium complex.

Some of the politicians who supported the tax wound up in political intensive care, and some were simply toe-tagged and carried out of political life. If history were about to repeat itself, certain elected officials did not intend to come out on the losing side.

Through some deft legal maneuvering, Chema overcame a late filing of the tax proposal with the State of Ohio.

*State Senator
Judy B. Sheerer*

*State Senator
Anthony Sinagra*

*State Representative
Patrick Sweeney*

*State Representative Jane L. Campbell and
Governor George Voinovich*

County Commissioners Mary O. Boyle, Virgil Brown, and James M. Petro (below).

State senators Anthony Sinagra and Judy Sheerer, and state representatives Patrick Sweeney, Jane Campbell, C. J. Prentiss, and Madeline Cain, kept the Gateway flame burning in the Ohio General Assembly.

Cuyahoga County commissioners continued their support as the project developed. A key moment came in March of 1992 when $75 million in bonds were issued for the arena, under commissioners Hagan, Boyle, and James M. Petro.

Another political figure with deep roots in Cleveland helped Gateway survive a later crisis. In early 1991, Chema visited Ohio Governor George Voinovich on several urgent matters related to Gateway. Projections showed that the proposed complex desperately needed $25 million in state capital improvement funds, a contingency loan of $12 million from the state, and the governor's tacit support of a sensitive property tax issue.

Voinovich, a former Cleveland mayor during whose term the notion of a domed stadium was originally conceived, agreed to lend his support.

In his opinion, it was imperative to move as quickly as possible to gain public support for the tax. Plagued by money problems, uncertain public support, and frequent changes in philosophy, Gateway was in constant danger of collapsing. "The whole deal died at least four times," Chema recalls. Yet when the polls opened at 6:30 a.m. on May 8, 1990, the tax was on the ballot.

The campaign had no money to conduct exit polls. But at campaign headquarters in the BP America building late that evening, Chema learned that the ratio of voting senior citizens was uniform throughout the county. In political parlance, that news translated into a hopeful sign.

An outpouring of senior votes in the suburbs would have signaled serious trouble for passage of the sin tax. It was 10:15 p.m., and Chema brightened.

By 11 p.m., only the slightest edge was being given to the passage of the tax. Cuyahoga County voters, it turned out, narrowly approved it — by 51.7 percent of the vote. The news, says Chema, "was a great relief."

The sweat and toil that preceded the public approval of the tax were about to pay off. No longer just a hope or a concept, Gateway was poised to rise from the ground and change the future of Cleveland.

Nine trustees were appointed in May of 1990 to govern the not-for-profit Gateway Economic Development Corporation of Greater Cleveland. Gateway would be supervised by a not-for-profit corporation rather than by a politically sensitive, quasi-governmental authority; that way, political stalemates and turf wars could be avoided. In a compromise worked out between White and Hagan, the city and the county each appointed four trustees to the board of the Corporation, with one trustee chosen by consensus.

OUTLINE PHOTOS: © PAUL CHRISTOPHER 1994

Patrick S. Parker, chairman of the Parker Hannifin Corporation, was named trustee chair. Other appointments included: David Abbott, Cuyahoga County administrator; Charles E. Brown, City of Cleveland finance director; Denise M. Fugo, president of City Life, Inc./Sammy's Restaurant; K.P. "Kip" Horsburgh Jr., president of Horsburgh & Scott Co.; Lawrence J. McManamon, international vice president, Great Lakes Area, Boilermakers, International Brotherhood, AFL-CIO; the Rev. Marvin A. McMickle, pastor of the Antioch Baptist Church and president of the Cleveland NAACP Chapter; Dr. Oscar E. Saffold, a dermatologist and medical director of Personal Physician Care of Ohio Inc.; and Edwina Moss, a civic activist.

"From the very beginning," Chema says, "the trustees followed Parker's lead, functioning as a corporate board, conducting

*Patrick Parker
Chairman, 1990-91*

*Stephen J. Strnisha
Trustee 1991-97*

*Below, left to right:
Lawrence J.
McManamon
Trustee 1990-97*

*Rev. Marvin A.
McMickle
Trustee 1990-97*

*Denise M. Fugo
Trustee 1990-92*

*K.P. "Kip"
Horsburgh, Jr.
Trustee 1990-97*

*Charles E. Brown
Trustee 1990-91*

itself as a business rather than as a political entity."

Appointed Gateway's executive director, Chema, in very short order and with no budget, had to set up offices and hire a top-notch staff capable of dealing with unforeseen obstacles and problems a project like Gateway would encounter while he continued to meet with key public officials to keep the Gateway ball rolling.

In November, 1990, an agreement between Cleveland, Cuyahoga County, and Gateway was unanimously approved by the County Commissioners and the City, authorizing the complex to be built at the Central Market site.

Simultaneously, trustees of the New Stadium Corporation, which owned the site, voted to merge with Gateway, and, by terminating the New Stadium Corporation, Mosier had fulfilled his obligation to Holmes. Later that year, Holmes would succumb to a fatal attack of a

nerve disease that had afflicted him for several years.

In December, the Cavaliers and Indians signed memoranda of intent, establishing the economic terms which formed the basis for later lease negotiations.

Another critical date lay ahead: a December 31 deadline to sell $148 million in three tax-exempt bond issues to finance the ballpark. If these construction bonds were not sold by that time, Gateway would lose a federal tax exemption, adding another $32 million to Gateway's price tag.

The bonds, rated good investment prospects by Moody's Investors Service, sold out in one day — December 18, 1990.

But it was not yet time to celebrate. The rest of the financing package needed to be in place before designs and construction timetables could be considered, and time was running out.

Greater Cleveland and its elected officials had done their part. It was time to get the private sector into the game.

The Plan —

The Corporate Players

Gateway exists because of the extraordinary public-private partnership that championed it. And while the public support has been well documented in the media, Gateway's private supporters are its unsung heroes.

Companies large and small contributed to the dream and the vision in countless ways: with time, with effort, with money. They donated office space and human resources, thinking time and volunteers. They purchased suites, club seats, and tickets. They contributed ideas and support.

Why these companies and the people who work for them did so much is no mystery. They believed the future would be better because of Gateway. It turns out they were right.

Yet, from the beginning, there were no guarantees that there would be a payoff for their hard work and determination. There was only the hope that they could make a difference.

Gateway: Blueprint Of The Future

Calfee, Halter & Griswold

When CH&G was called upon to assist Gateway, it was not possible to fathom the many challenges that would have to be met to successfully complete this complex and multi-faceted project.

In its dual role as Bond Counsel and Special Counsel to Gateway, CH&G applied its creativity and legal expertise to solving those challenges. In developing the financing package for the Gateway facilities, negotiating with the Cavs and Indians, and working with the many governmental and private organizations involved in the project, CH&G helped Gateway redefine the meaning of public-private partnerships — a concept CH&G began defining a decade earlier.

CH&G's efforts on the project began in early 1990 by helping Gateway to secure Letters of Intent from the Indians and the Cavs. These letters, which highlighted the teams' commitment to the new sports facilities, were important components in the passage of the luxury tax in Cuyahoga County.

CH&G's public finance team went to work, accomplishing a series of complicated financing transactions, culminating in the sale of nearly $150 million of tax-exempt bonds on December 27, 1990.

The financing team found itself working under extraordinary time pressures: The law permitting tax-exempt financing was set to expire on December 31, 1990. Failure to meet this deadline would have meant the collapse of the intricate financing plan. CH&G's attorneys also developed unique escrow account arrangements for the bond proceeds to satisfy tax laws and credit markets, and negotiated several unique credit arrangements to keep Gateway's fast-track construction process on schedule.

CH&G began the arduous task of drafting and negotiating a series of agreements with both the Indians and the Cavaliers, beginning with Memorandums of Understanding. These agreements established the responsibilities of the various parties for the leasing, financing, management and construction of the ballpark, the arena, the common areas and the parking facilities. Signed in the last half of 1991, these formed the blueprint for construction of the Gateway complex as well as defining legal relationships among among all parties.

Just as CH&G is helping to define Cleveland's future, it also played an active role in developing new financial strategies to take Cleveland from default to fiscal integrity under then-Mayor George Voinovich in the early '80s. They engineered strategies for public-private partnerships to boost Greater Cleveland's economy.

CH&G's contribution to Cleveland both in the '80s and '90s has been its ability to take complicated concepts, break them into manageable parts and reassemble the parts into successful, measurable results. CH&G has been doing that for nearly 90 years.

From CH&G's participation in righting Cleveland's financial ship to the success of Gateway, the firm has played an integral role in shaping the vision that has generated the national respect that Cleveland now enjoys. CH&G is proud to be part of Cleveland's renaissance, and a part of its history.

Allen Holmes exemplified corporate Cleveland's dedication to the cause. Taking over the domed stadium leadership from William MacDonald, former president of Ohio Bell Telephone Co., Holmes, managing partner of Jones Day, was uniquely suited to lead the charge. "He was brilliant, politically astute, and forged strong relationships," says Frank Mosier. Albert Ratner likens Holmes' influence in Cleveland to the Big 10 adage that says "if you want to go to the Rose Bowl, you go through Michigan. In Cleveland, if you wanted to get something done, you went through Allen Holmes."

As the Greater Cleveland Domed Stadium Corporation's first chairman and president, Holmes was surrounded by a galaxy of high-powered executives and professionals — J. Robert Killpack, president of National City Corp., headed the finance committee; Thomas A. Commes, senior vice president for finance of the Sherwin-Williams Co., was in charge of the site committee; Mosier took charge as chairman of the facilities committee; and Larry Robinson, chairman of J.B. Robinson Jewelers, headed the marketing and community relations committee. Others included Mary Ann

Allen C. Holmes, arguably Cleveland's most influential individual in the 1980s, exemplified the civic leadership which sustained the drive for a new stadium. Although confined to a wheelchair by 1986, shortly after this photograph at the 1st Annual meeting of the Domed Stadium Corporation was taken, he continued to fight tirelessly for the dome.

Jorgenson of the law firm Squire, Sanders & Dempsey, Robert R. Broadbent of The Higbee Company, and Jeffrey I. Friedman of Associated Estates Corp. One after another, these and other people involved in the Corporation represented the best and brightest minds of Cleveland's board rooms.

From the beginning, dome proponents sought help from the city's most powerful and unique corporate resource — Cleveland Tomorrow. As Greater Cleveland's

Thompson, Hine and Flory

Building Gateway took more than bricks, mortar, steel,
and glass. The real work began well before the first shovel
of dirt was turned, when business and community leaders
forged an essential public-private partnership.

Only then could Gateway enter into several innovative construction agreements to ensure a timely project completion. One of Cleveland's oldest and most respected law firms, Thompson, Hine and Flory, played a key role in both of these efforts.

Experts in public finance and construction law, TH&F first helped to move the Gateway project forward in 1989 by working with community leaders and investment bankers, serving as underwriter's counsel to secure nearly $150 million in tax-exempt bond sales, completed in late 1990. The levy campaign, chaired by one of the firm's partners, Oliver "Pudge" Henkel, assisted in making the financing possible.

The financing secured, TH&F developed a coordinated series of design, consulting and construction contracts specifically tailored to Gateway's size and complexity. Because Gateway's design, bidding and construction was performed in phases, with more than 65 contracts negotiated or prepared for bid, TH&F utilized a "Project Counsel" concept, which included labor relations and construction claims resolution.

With TH&F's assistance, Gateway entered into several innovative agreements that have set national precedents for the construction industry. Incorporated into every construction contract, a Minority and Female Business Enterprise policy set a new affirmative action standard by carefully tailoring project MBE/FBE goals to availability and contractors' documented efforts to maximize minority- and female-owned business participation.

Another unique agreement developed by the firm was the project labor agreement — a contract with the Cleveland building trades calling for the use of all union labor in exchange for a no-strike commitment, the first ever on a publicly-funded project.

The theme of cooperation and prompt dispute resolution ensured project completion without work stoppage or delay. Gateway officials found TH&F extremely responsive to all their needs and credit the thorough preparation and negotiation of contracts with the project's low incidence of construction and labor disputes.

TH&F's legal expertise has benefited a number of other Cleveland projects, including The Galleria, Tower City Center, Society Center, the Marriott Hotel at Society Center, Renaissance on Playhouse Square, BP America Headquarters, and One Cleveland Center.

In addition to construction law and public finance, TH&F maintains a strong litigation practice and expertise in the area of administrative law and government contracts, antitrust and trade regulation, banking, commercial law and bankruptcy, closely held and emerging businesses, corporate and securities law, employee benefits, environmental regulation, estate planning and probate, foundations and exempt organizations, health care, intellectual property, international law, labor, employment and workers' compensation, real estate, taxation, transportation and admiralty law.

TH&F has a distinguished history of community involvement. Since the days of Walter Flory's work to improve Cleveland city government through the formation of the Citizens League, and his service as a founding father of the Cleveland Play House, the firm's attorneys have carried out this tradition of public service.

premier economic development entity, made up of the top executives from 50 of the region's largest corporations, Cleveland Tomorrow has played a pivotal role in the remarkable revitalization of Cleveland. The reception its membership gave to the proposed dome was a warm one indeed.

"To a person, the corporate community was in favor of the new stadium," says Richard Shatten, former executive director of Cleveland Tomorrow.

In the mid '80s, Shatten and other Cleveland Tomorrow staff rolled up their sleeves and pitched in long hours. By his own reckoning, 75 percent of Shatten's time from February of 1987 to June of 1990 was spent on Gateway-related business.

But Cleveland Tomorrow invested more than just sweat.

Capitalized through Cleveland Tomorrow, the Cleveland Development Partnership loaned

The Founders Club

One of the last pieces of financing necessary to complete Gateway was the sale of $20 million in luxury seating. The funds raised were used throughout the ballpark's construction. On the walls of Jacobs Field are 24 plaques recognizing the purchasers of ballpark suites whose civic spirit led them to make a major commitment to Gateway.

American Greetings

Forest City Enterprises

Ambassador Milton Wolf

Arter & Hadden

BP America

Baker & Hostetler

Blue Cross/Blue Shield
    of Ohio

Cleveland-Cliffs Inc.

East Ohio Gas Company

Eaton Co.

Ernst & Young

The Crawford Fitting Co.

General Electric

The Glidden Company

J. Walter Thompson

Ford Motor Co.

Jones, Day, Reavis &
    Pogue

M.A. Hanna Company

McDonald & Company

National City Bank

Ameritech

Parker Hannifin

The Plain Dealer
    Publishing Co.

RPM, Inc.

Sherwin-Williams

Society Bank

Squire, Sanders &
    Dempsey

Huntington Banks

Centerior Energy Corp.

TRW

WWWE Radio

With 50,000 watts of power, 3WE has heralded the comeback of the City of Cleveland to
a listening audience in 35 states and half of
Canada.

With a vision of growth for Cleveland's downtown, and realizing the financial impact a new sports and entertainment complex would have on the entire Greater Cleveland community, 3WE became an early proponent of the Gateway project.

3WE took the initiative and provided citizens of Cuyahoga County with a forum for discussion of the Gateway issue. Representatives of various county agencies discussed the planned stadium and arena project with the public, helping build a consensus for Gateway.

Now that Gateway is a reality, 3WE joined the complex in taking Cleveland back to the future with a time capsule for the next century, buried under Gateway Plaza in 1994, scheduled to be opened in the year 2064.

3WE Radio knows a lot about history. Its location on the radio dial dates back to 1923 when it operated as WTAM on a 1,500-watt transmitter. In the early years, the station began its public service and community programming with live radio coverage of the 1924 Republican National Convention at Cleveland's Public Hall. In 1928, the station began play-by-play broadcasts of Cleveland Indians games from League Park.

About that time, WTAM was sold to the Cleveland Electric Illuminating Company and the Van Sweringen brothers, Oris and Mantis, the developers of the Terminal Tower. WTAM became a 50,000-watt powerhouse, and the rest, as they say, is history.

In 1965, NBC took control of the station and renamed it WKYC. Seven years later, Cleveland businessman Nick Mileti bought the station and changed the name to its current call letters. During the next 18 years, the station would see more ownership changes. At one point, 3WE was the radio home of three professional sports teams: the Indians, Browns, and Cavaliers.

Since 1990, 3WE has been owned by Booth Broadcasting of Detroit. The station, "Newsradio 1100 3WE," operates Cleveland's only 24-hour radio newsroom. Awards from the Ohio Associated Press won by 3WE include best outstanding news operation and regularly scheduled sports, best investigative and enterprise reporting, and best broadcast writing.

3WE is making an impact not only in the newsroom, but in Cleveland and around the country as well. When Hurricane Andrew devastated southern Florida, 3WE was quick to respond with Operation Homestead, a joint effort with the Salvation Army of Cleveland. The station opened its phone lines and Clevelanders opened their hearts, sending 3WE talk show host Lee Kirk to Florida with truckloads of goods. And in July 1993, 3WE joined the national Flood Relief Radio Network to aid victims of the devastating floods that hit the Midwest. The station devoted an entire day to an on-air auction, with proceeds benefiting the Red Cross Flood Relief Fund.

In Cleveland, 3WE has become synonymous with Coats for Kids. The efforts of 3WE and Cleveland charities and businesses to provide a warm coat for every child in need has resulted in more than 177,500 coats being collected during 3WE's years of involvement.

Whether on the dial or in the streets, 3WE is a valuable city partner, helping to make Cleveland a better place.

Gateway $28 million. They also assisted in lease negotiations, wrote checks to facilitate the development process, and helped organize the early sale of suites. It was, in fact, during a Cleveland Tomorrow strategy planning meeting for the excise tax campaign that the name "Gateway" was picked from 20 possible selections posted on a flip chart.

A number of local business leaders stepped forward to carry the flag for the Gateway concept, often at critical times when, without their help, the project might have collapsed. One of these was James Biggar, chairman and CEO of Nestle Enterprises, Inc., as well as a former chairman of Cleveland Tomorrow.

At one point, when the sale of suites to local companies became an imperative building block in Gateway financing, Biggar joined Patrick Parker and Edward Brandon, chairman and CEO of National City

*B*oth BP America, through the involvement of Frank Mosier (above left), and Parker Hannifin Corporation, thanks to Patrick Parker, put their corporate jets at the disposal of the Gateway board and staff as they examined premier stadiums throughout North America.

Corporation, in persuading local executives to invest in 10-year, prepaid luxury ballpark seating. Twenty-five Cleveland companies made 10-year commitments to leasing luxury ballpark suites, at costs of $724,000 to $874,000.

With the additional sale of three- and five-year leases, two-thirds of the 126 suites were leased in less than four months, faster than anyone thought possible. Biggar was later appointed chairman of Gateway Economic Development Corporation.

"Buying a suite was not the issue," says Biggar. "The issue was investing in Cleveland's future. We just asked, 'What kind of city do you want to have?'"

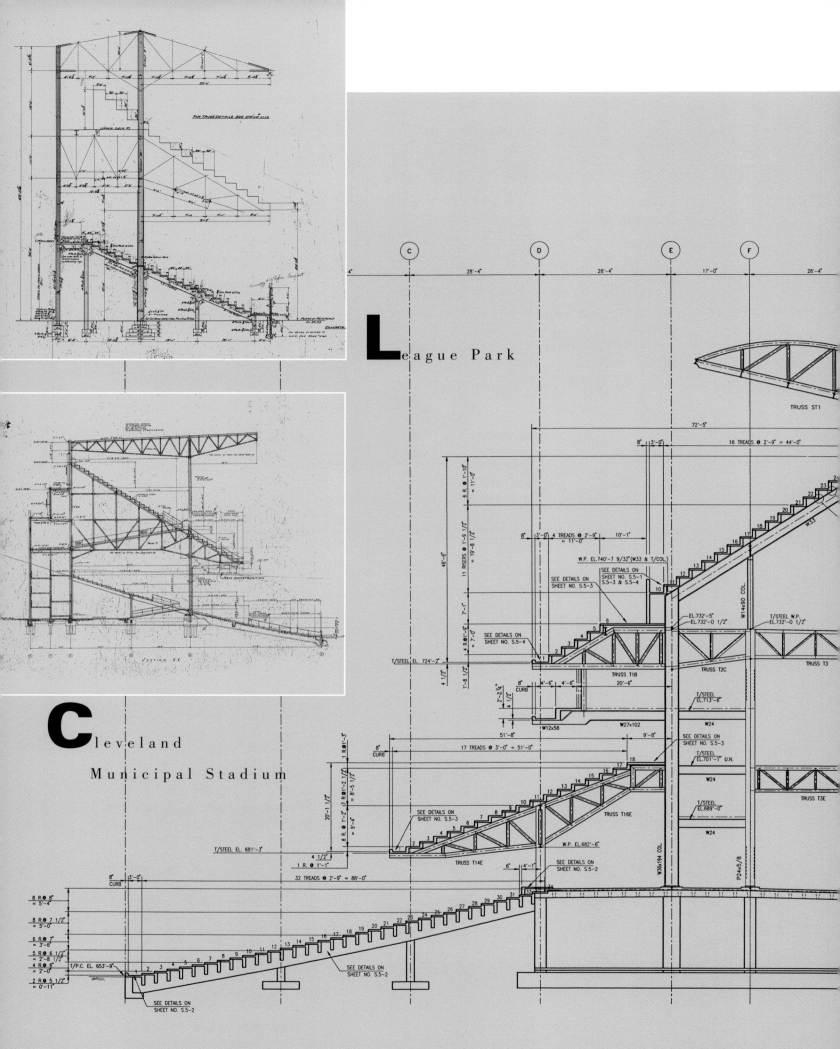

League Park

Cleveland
Municipal Stadium

SECTION THRU CLUB SEAT

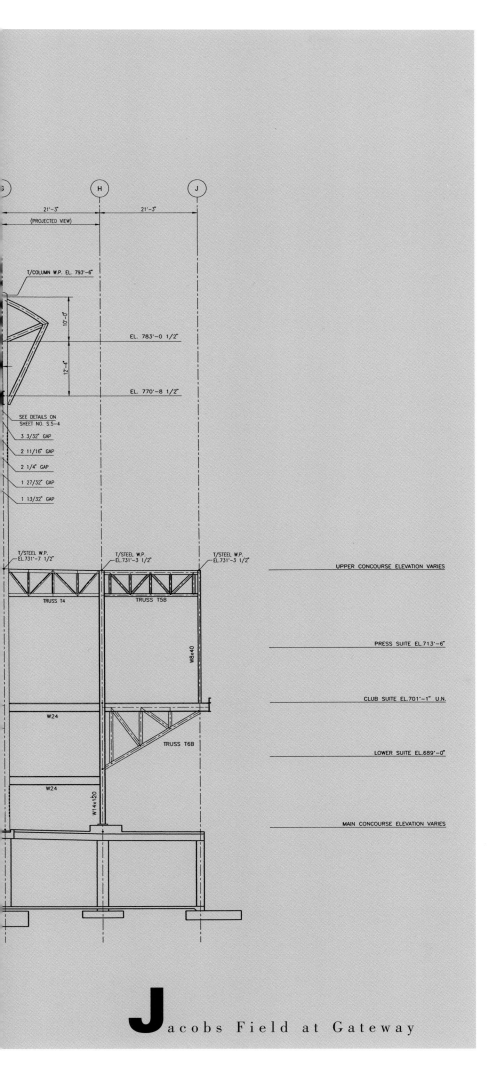

Jacobs Field at Gateway

In just over a century, Cleveland's ballparks have come full circle.

And Osborn Engineering is a part of this legacy. Beginning with the intimacy of League Park, followed by the awesome dimensions of Muny Stadium, they have put their "fingerprint" on Jacobs Field, combining intimacy with modern technology.

Shortly after the turn of the century, ballpark design evolved from wood into steel and concrete stadium construction. Osborn's founder, Frank C. Osborn, parlayed his aptitude for dealing with large steel structures into innovative designs accommodating this structural transition. Osborn quickly became the national pastime's foremost designer, with early accomplishments including the rebuilding of New York's historic Polo Grounds.

Osborn pioneered the development of "second generation" stadiums, such as Washington D.C.'s RFK Stadium and Pittsburgh's Three Rivers Stadium, which incorporated unobstructed views, movable seats, and multi-purpose stadium venues.

Osborn Engineering has been instrumental to the design of such collegiate landmarks as the Universities of Notre Dame and Michigan football stadiums. Today, Osborn's innovative spirit carries on into a second century of providing design excellence.

Countdown To

Opening Day

While

the Public

and Private

support was

crucial to the

success of

the project,

ultimately,

an agreement

between

Gateway and

the Indians

was the

foundation

upon which

the hopes

and dreams

of Cleveland

would be

built.

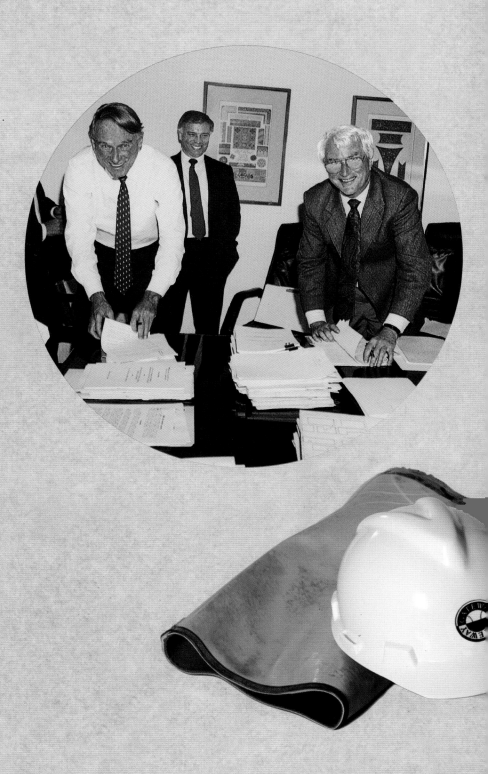

Until the Indians officially accepted the ballpark as their new home, nothing could be taken for granted. If Cleveland lost the Indians, the emotional blow, to say nothing of the financial impact, would be devastating. The city would lose part of its history, its tradition, its identity — its very fiber.

Gateway was under pressure to obtain an unprecedented financial commitment from the Indians, which included terms that would keep them in Cleveland for a long time. The Indians wanted terms which were competitive with lucrative offers from other cities courting them. And both sides demanded an out if financing went awry.

But these economic issues were resolved relatively quickly. The real issue on the table was security for the club – and how Gateway was going to provide it.

Chema knew the main sticking point was "assuring the team that once we went forward, we would build the ballpark."

The fact that Gateway had two primary tenants to deal with further complicated negotiations; neither the Indians nor the Cavaliers wanted to subsidize the other's facility if something went wrong. Gateway needed to satisfy both teams that the financing plan would carry the arena as well as the ballpark.

On July 3, 1991, the Gateway Board of Trustees approved a 20-year deal with the Tribe which dovetailed into successful negotiations with the Cavs.

In December, 1991, the Cavs signed a 30-year arena lease.

Together, the two teams committed more than $225 million, far exceeding any previous agreement between a professional sports team and a sports facility.

The Gateway Board had already given unanimous approval to the Gateway design plan.

It was time to dig down and build.

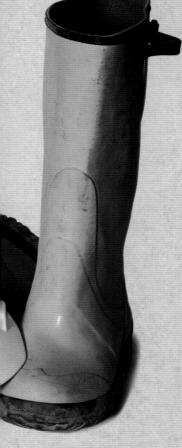

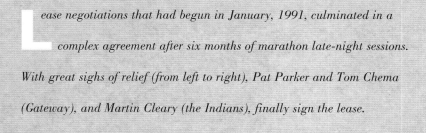

Lease negotiations that had begun in January, 1991, culminated in a complex agreement after six months of marathon late-night sessions. With great sighs of relief (from left to right), Pat Parker and Tom Chema (Gateway), and Martin Cleary (the Indians), finally sign the lease.

In selecting architectural and design firms, Gateway took an innovative approach, spurning traditional wisdom which said that a single firm should be selected to oversee design of the entire complex. Gateway officials were convinced that a team approach, using different design and architectural firms, with their varied experience and interests, would enhance each others' work to bring in the best possible design.

They further felt that a division of design responsibilities would foster an unprecedented system of beneficial checks and balances.

After requests for bids were sent out and proposals submitted, Gateway officials took a deep breath, and, with bold determination to "do it their way," hired three "lead" design firms, each with different responsibilities.

Kansas City-based Hellmuth, Obata & Kassabaum, Inc. (HOK) was the choice for the ballpark. One of the top ballpark design firms in the world, HOK brought a wealth of experience to the task, having recently designed Chicago's Comiskey Park and Baltimore's Camden Yards.

The arena was awarded to Ellerbe Becket, Inc., a firm with extensive experience in arena design. The Boston Garden and the renovation of Madison Square Garden are two of their key credits.

Sasaki Associates, Inc., was selected as leader of the site design team. Serving as the master planner and urban designer of the project, Sasaki had responsibility for determining where and how the different elements of Gateway could best fit into the tight urban landscape.

When the designs were complete, there was yet another step — determining how much it would cost to build what the designers submitted. This task went to the Gilbane Building Co., which made sure the plans could be realized at a reasonable cost.

Committee meetings and public hearings encouraged community participation to build consensus. The design was refined to reflect the urban environment into which Gateway would be placed.

The Gateway Board of Trustees and Executive Director Thomas Chema travelled to many modern ballparks throughout the United States to evaluate and distill the very best design features of each facility.

Of the three new American League ballparks built in the early 1990s, Cleveland's, with 42,500 seats, is the smallest, hearkening back to League Park's "intimate dimensions." Oriole Park at Camden Yards has 48,000 seats, while Comiskey Park in Chicago has 44,321.

HOK presented hundreds of models and drawings, perfecting original design components as well as those inspired by other facilities, before the final selection was made.

PHOTOS: MODELS, COURTESY OF HOK

Gateway: Blueprint Of The Future

This may look like a rock, but guess again! It's actually a baseball, dating back to the 1880s, and was one of the artifacts unearthed by the Museum of Natural History archeological dig of the Gateway site.

Independence Excavating

When the late Sam DiGeronimo came to the United States in 1928 from the region of Abruzzi in Italy, little did he know the major impact his life's work would have on Cleveland.

DiGeronimo and his son, Don, founded Independence Excavating 35 years ago. Sam started small; his was a family business and it was to stay that way as his five sons joined him in his work. Today, the firm, one of the largest excavators in the country, was the site-preparer for Gateway's ballpark and arena complex.

Sam built houses and small commercial buildings while Don diversified IE's business from residential and small-business contractors into the commercial excavation trades. By the late 1970s, IE had become a leading commercial excavator. In 1971, the company had to surmount major obstacles in overcoming Don's unexpected death from cancer. Now, Don's brothers — Vic, Rich, Bob, and Tony — keep the family business dream alive, boasting annual sales of more than $25 million. From their Schaaf Road offices, the DiGeronimo brothers oversee a company which, since 1971, has been involved in the majority of building projects in downtown Cleveland: Justice Center, Park Center/Reserve Square, Medical Mutual Building/One Cleveland Center, Renaissance Building, Bank One, Cleveland State University Convocation Center and Science and Health buildings, Eaton Building, Society Tower, and Rock and Roll Hall of Fame and Museum.

The company's expertise in heavy foundation excavation, highway site

But before the heavy equipment and construction workers moved onto the site to build what the designers envisioned, there was some serious scientific digging to be done.

In November of 1991, a team of archaeologists from the Cleveland Museum of Natural History dug 15 areas at the site. They found stone points, flint chips, and a cooking pot from an Indian village dating to 1200-1300 A.D. They also unearthed utensils, cookware, and other artifacts used by Clevelanders who lived on the site in the 19th century.

On January 6, 1992, the Sheriff Cold Storage Building, the last major structure on the Gateway site, came down with a mighty implosion (see next page). Excavation for the ballpark began the following week.

(see next page)

It was the biggest excavation job in Cleveland history. Independence Excavating, Inc., took on this monumental task. A portable stone crusher, their own technology, was used on the site to break old foundations and roadways into various sizes which were then used for aggregate in paving and landscaping at Gateway.

preparation, sewer construction, erosion control, and aggregate crushing and recycling have taken IE across Ohio and to other areas in the United States.

IE began work on Gateway in January, 1992. The initial project involved clearing 20 acres of downtown property. Not only did the company clear the land, haul the dirt from the project site, and prepare the site for construction, but it also utilized its portable and stationary concrete-recycling processes. It was the first time this innovative recycling process was used on a downtown project.

As part of the major excavation for Gateway, IE constructed a temporary earth retention system to protect Carnegie Avenue and Ontario Street utilities during Gateway construction. The company also was involved in building the storm and sanitary sewer system and backfilling the surrounding grounds so that landscaping and walkways could be installed. After the ballpark was erected, IE completed the exterior site finishes before opening day, including exterior paving, granite curbs and steps, landscaping planters, trees and irrigation, electrical lighting, fencing, parking lot construction, security walls, and the placement of donor brick pavers around the Bob Feller statue in Gateway's Indian Square.

Because Sam DiGeronimo was a proponent of education, his sons have provided scholarship money to local high schools and vocational programs. The company promotes programs sponsored by various construction trade organizations that further the education of construction industry professionals, and supports a variety of charitable causes that benefit Greater Cleveland.

How quickly we forget! The new ballpark was not built "overnight." Site demolition actually began in June, 1987!

John Loyd (right), project manager for Gateway, and Jeff Appelbaum of Thompson, Hine and Flory, discuss where excavation will begin. They are standing next to the "earth mover" that turned the first earth on the site.

PHOTOS: IMPLOSION, MORT TUCKER PHOTOGRAPHY ©1994; CONSTRUCTION SITE, SKYVIEW PHOTOGRAPHY ©1994; SMALL PHOTO, LEFT, COURTESY TH&F.

Reminiscent of a Hollywood movie, the series of dramatic photos (above) show the implosion of the Sheriff Cold Storage Building, the last physical reminder that Jacobs Field sits on what was once home to the bustling Sheriff Street Market which opened in 1891. Ironically, that same year the Spiders inaugurated League Park.

The market closed in 1936, which marked the beginning of ferocious Tribe pitching, culminating in a 1948 world championship. Seventeen-year old Bob Feller, the catalyst, debuted in August, 1936, striking out 15 St. Louis Browns, one shy of the American League record, which he broke three weeks later by ringing up 17 against the Philadelphia Athletics at League Park.

Gateway: Blueprint Of The Future

Donley's, Inc.

Ernest F. Donley and his three brothers founded the Donley Brothers Company in 1896. Reorganized in 1941 to specialize in cast-in-place concrete, today it's one of Ohio's leading and most highly-respected construction firms.

Throughout its years of operation, Donley's has executed more than $800 million in new and renovation construction. The Donley philosophy, carried out today by company President Terrance K. Donley, grandson of the founder, demands quality in service, performance, management, and client relations. Adherence to these operating principles by a staff of 200 managers, engineers, technicians, and skilled craftsmen is responsible for their success.

Donley's completed all cast-in-place structural concrete for Jacobs Field, and executed all interior general trades for the 53,000 square-foot, four-story Indians Administration Building, the Terrace Club restaurant and bar, Club Lounge, 126 loges, and all ballpark public areas. Donley's also completed the construction of the 1,100-vehicle off-site adjacent parking garage.

The company is not only proud of its work at Gateway, but also of its impressive job-safety record. Throughout the construction phase, it maintained a high safety rating. A dedicated safety coordinator made certain that on-site construction personnel utilized proper

Gateway: Blueprint Of The Future

After long years of effort, the earth on the Gateway site was finally being shoved, pushed, piled and removed to make room for a gleaming new sports and entertainment complex.

In April, excavation began on the arena. One month later, the foundation for the ballpark was poured by Donley's, Inc. Incredibly, all the work would get done ahead of schedule and up to — or exceeding — quality requirements.

Suddenly the office workers driving through downtown every day became aware that Gateway was beginning to take shape before their very eyes. The project literally came up out of the ground when the first structural steel beams were erected at the ballpark by the Kilroy Structural Steel Co., using 1,500 tons of steel produced locally by USS Kobe of Lorain, Ohio.

The ballpark's sunken playing field presented special challenges to Donley's construction crew. Because the dugouts and field-level suites are five feet below water level, the site had to be "de-watered" before Donley's could install a "hydrostatic" concrete slab. Six hundred feet long and five feet thick, the slab curves between first and third bases.

safety measures and maintained a safe work environment. Donley's commitment to safety has earned it outstanding safety ratings with the Ohio Bureau of Workers' Compensation.

Donley's also took the lead at Gateway to ensure that all minority- and female-owned enterprises were incorporated into management, sharing responsibility for the project's completion.

Donley's served as general contractor for reconstruction of the War Memorial on Mall A. The existing statue, "The Fountain of Eternal Life," was removed, refurbished with an aqua epoxy coating, and reinstalled within a new granite fountain and reflecting pond.

Other of Donley's noteworthy Cleveland-area projects include the $20-million Allstate Insurance Data Center, the archive and rare book library building for the Western Reserve Historical Society, and University Hospitals patient tower. Donley's projects dot the landscape around Ohio and as far east as Baltimore, where it worked on a construction project for Johns Hopkins Hospital.

As a respected leader in the construction trades for nearly a century, Donley's has left its imprint on many local communities across Ohio and several other states. Specializing in construction of monumentals, institutions, industrial plants and parking garages, Donley's has come a long way from its roots as a small building specialties manufacturer. From a showcase for America's favorite pastime and showpiece for Cleveland's future, to a home for artifacts from Cleveland's history, Donley's is helping to build the foundation for a thriving city.

Cleveland Electric Illuminating Company

The real "power" behind Jacobs Field is measured in kilowatt hours, not RBI's.

Without electricity, night games, the scoreboard, the instant replays, the hot food, and the signature light towers would be missing from the Gateway scene. Since Charles Brush invented the arc light and made Cleveland the site of America's first outdoor electric street lighting by illuminating Public Square, CEI has been an integral part of Cleveland history.

Brush founded the Brush Electric Light & Power Company, one of CEI's predecessors. When his crews began stringing power lines in Cleveland in 1881, his service area was one-quarter of a square mile and included only 88 street lamps. In 1986, CEI merged with Toledo Edison to form Centerior Energy Corporation, which serves more than 3 million people in Northern Ohio.

Centerior's 7,000 employees do their part to make Northern Ohio a world-class place to live and work. The company has developed numerous energy management programs to help customers use electricity wisely to keep energy costs down. Other corporate priorities include an aggressive economic development program, environmental initiatives, and a strong commitment to its civic responsibilities as a good corporate neighbor. One of its guiding principles is "to balance its stewardship of natural resources with society's need for a safe and reliable supply of electricity."

Gateway: Blueprint Of The Future

PHOTO: ©1994 PAUL CHRISTOPHER

This commitment goes back to the 1920s when CEI and Toledo Edison voluntarily installed pollution-control devices on each new generating unit as it was built.

Since 1977, the company has spent more than $1 billion adhering to its environmental commitment. And these efforts continue with such programs as CEI's Arbor Day Program, aimed at creating environmental awareness in Cleveland Public School third-graders by giving them tree seedlings to plant. Since 1986, about 50,000 seedlings have been distributed.

Other civic work includes donating a 35-foot van to the Red Cross for the agency's Bloodmobile program, and creating for the city of Cleveland a quarter-acre park in the Flats, Riverbend City Side Garden, developed for CEI by CLEAN-LAND, OHIO. CEI and Toledo Edison turn over a portion of their annual revenues to the Centerior Foundation, which distributes more than $1 million to several hundred area organizations and endeavors.

CEI ConserVan, an electric vehicle, increases awareness of electric technology, particularly electric vehicles, and it is part of the company's overall strategy to promote economic development in Cleveland. CEI recently hosted the premier electric formula race in the world — the Cleveland Electric Grand Prix. The race, part of the 1994 Cleveland Grand Prix, featured electric-powered Formula Lighting cars built by students from U.S. universities.

The new $30 million Horizon Substation in the Flats, with its state-of-the-art technology, will provide safe and reliable electricity to Gateway and to present and future downtown customers. CEI is a part of Cleveland's history, and is a part of its future. As Cleveland moves into the 21st century, CEI will be there to light the way.

All Erection & Crane Rental Corporation

Look, up in the sky, it's a bird, it's a plane! No, it's All Erection & Crane. Sounds far-fetched, but most of the giant cranes that towered high above Gateway belong to Cleveland-based All Erection & Crane Rental Corp.

From the the beginning, All Erection equipment was on the job, hoisting thousands of steel girders, setting tons of precast concrete in place, and erecting the ballpark lights and scoreboard.

No easy task, considering the logistics involved in such a massive project, but one that contractors who relied on All Erection's equipment took in stride. Donley's, Kilroy Steel Erectors, Dunlop and Johnson, Precast Service, Forest City Erectors, and R.W. Sidley — each used cranes, aerial work platforms, boom trucks, forklifts, dozers, loaders and backhoes provided by All Erection.

An industry leader, All Erection began in 1965 as the dream of three brothers. Mike, Larry, and Jake Liptak had the idea of leasing heavy-duty construction equipment to area contractors. What started as a one-crane company today has 10 branch offices east of the Mississippi, more than 500 employees, and thousands of pieces of machinery.

Apart from leasing equipment, All Erection also acts as a dealer for a number of manufacturers, and provides specialized carrier services for heavy or oversized equipment and structures, such as those "wide loads" often seen traveling along the highways.

Over the years, AE has been involved in a number of Cleveland's more monumental construction projects, such as the BP America building, Society Center, Tower City, The Cleveland State University Convocation Center, and, most recently, North Coast Harbor, and the Rock and Roll Hall of Fame and Museum. The company views its contribution to the city's renaissance with great pride.

All Erection also has participated in civic programs fostering the city's ongoing development. Recently, the company donated one of its cranes to the Cleveland Police Department to aid in the construction of a training building for the department's S.W.A.T. team.

Thanks to All Erection, area residents, visitors and sports fans not only enjoy Gateway today, but reap the benefits of the company's continuing efforts to help build a better Cleveland for tomorrow.

Gateway: Blueprint Of The Future

Although it was easy to see progress, it was not so easy to see the synchronization required to fit each design and construction component into a master plan which included as many as 1,400 workers on the site at the same time.

Huber, Hunt & Nichols, Inc., was the construction manager, marshalling the contractors and sub-contractors, the workers and their machines, into a cohesive unit. ColeJon Corporation and IEA Electric Corporation were its "Lieutenants".

Jim Biggar, an engineer by background, a CEO by vocation, and Chairman of Gateway's board, played a key role in keeping construction of the ballpark and arena on time and on schedule. "My job was to see that there was trust between parties," he says. "The hitches were solved in job meetings, not in the newspaper."

A unique labor agreement was managed by James Marniella of the labor-relations firm of Marniella & Associates, Inc. Recognizing the importance of Gateway to its members and to Greater Cleveland's future, northern Ohio trade unions pledged that construction would not be interrupted, and the April 4, 1994, deadline would be met. In return Gateway was an all union project.

PHOTOS: THIS PAGE AND PREVIOUS PAGE ERIC MULL, ALL ERECTION & CRANE RENTAL CORP.

This lattice boom crawler requires four to five operators one full week to assemble, and remained on the site for over a year. The booms extended as high as 350 feet, and the small arm, or jib, reached an additional 50 feet.

Some All Erection operators have made more than 500,000 lifts in their careers, and have been with the company since it was founded twenty-five years ago.

Huber, Hunt & Nichols

Gateway needed a firm that would manage the construction of the ballpark, and bring it in on-time and on-budget.

And Huber, Hunt & Nichols said they could, and they did. No strangers to complicated construction projects, they originally gained their reputation converting local Indianapolis manufacturing plants from war production to civilian production following World War II.

Arber J. Huber, Paul B. Hunt and Harry Nichols came to Indianapolis in 1944 to build plants for war production. Huber and Nichols left, and Hunt carried on as sole owner.

After making a name for himself with his efficient, quality conversions, Hunt left his company in the care of his son, Robert, an engineering graduate of Case Institute of Technology, with a graduate degree from M.I.T.

Robert realized the company's resources could not continue to be dedicated to one market segment, and so he planned diversification into office buildings, hospitals, arenas, hotels, and research facilities which became standard components of HH&N. Now, HH&N is a recognized leader in the construction industry as a construction manger and general contractor, with offices in Phoenix, Dallas, and Branchburg, New Jersey.

HH&N has a total of 33 mass-seating unique facilities to its credit: America West Arena in Phoenix; Arrowhead Pond of Anaheim; Alamo Dome in San Antonio; Sabres Arena in Buffalo; Northwest Arena in Vancouver; Superdome in New Orleans; Hoosier Dome in Indianapolis; Riverfront Stadium in Cincinnati; Joe Robbie Stadium in Miami; and Bradley Center in Milwaukee.

Huber, Hunt & Nichols, with a calendar of projects like Jacobs Field in other cities, will continue to help build the future of sports and entertainment in America.

Can you imagine having to co-ordinate the placement of every structural element, every work force, and the order in which they occurred? HH&N had to do more than imagine: they engineered each of those components daily even before the first worker arrived on the site.

From the upper left-hand corner, clockwise, is a pictorial "evolution of a ballpark". The first photo was taken January, 1993; the next April 4, 1993; and the last, August 24, 1992.

From the moment the first shovel of earth was turned, Gateway set a new standard for female and minority participation. In August of 1993, 84 women construction workers were on the job, more than on any other project in the country. Gateway was the first project to reach a 15-year-old federal hiring goal of 6.9 percent female participation on a construction site. Further, Gateway easily met its goal of 22.6 percent minority participation from the building trades, exceeding national norms and federal guidelines.

Bob Decker was Huber, Hunt & Nichols' project manager. A big, gruff figure with a mule skinner's voice, Decker's orders and exhortations could be heard even above the din of the work.

Faced with deadlines that could not be renegotiated under any circumstances, Huber, Hunt, & Nichols ran their site as if on a military campaign.

The enemy was time. The ballpark had to be ready for the Indians home opener on April 4, 1994. It wasn't easy, but the good guys won.

Gateway: Blueprint Of The Future

The contrast between the lush green Kentucky Blue Grass and the rich Tennessee red clay make an impressive visual statement, dramatically depicting one facet of why Jacobs Field is heralded as one of the most beautiful ballparks in America.

The birth of the home plate area underscores the geometric precision necessary in laying out the playing field. S. W. Franks Construction Company chose specific state-of-the-art materials to best fit exact needs. For instance, the home plate area was built with more than 20 tons of a hard blue clay called "Pro-mound". Selected for its durability and ability to stand up to abuse by the cleats on a player's shoes, Pro-mound also was used for the pitchers mound and bullpens.

In August and September of 1993, S.W. Franks crews worked around the clock, coordinating their efforts with other construction taking place simultaneously.

These early photos show workers installing the various sub-surfaces for the field's drainage system and root zone, composed of a special growing medium for the grass.

PHOTOS: THIS PAGE AND PREVIOUS COURTESY OF S.W. FRANKS COMPANY, BY SKYVIEW PHOTOGRAPHY

Gateway: Blueprint Of The Future

Play Ball!

Now Jacobs

Field is an

accomplished

fact, and what

a fact it is.

Poised for the first

pitch at Jacobs Field,

U.S. President Bill Clinton signals catcher Sandy Alomar. Cheering

him on to his left: Cuyahoga County Commissioner Tim

Hagan, Cleveland Mayor Mike White, White House

photographer, Ohio Governor George Voinovich, Cuyahoga

County Commissioners Mary Boyle and Jim Petro, Indians

Hall of Famer Bob Feller, and, to the right, Gateway

Chairman Jim Biggar, former Ohio Governor Dick Celeste,

Gateway Executive Director Tom Chema, and Indians owner

Dick Jacobs.

Fans stand as the Cleveland Orchestra brass section

begins the National Anthem (above right).

Jacobs Field, Opening Day, April 4, 1994.

Architecturally, the ballpark fits into the cityscape of Cleveland like a ball in a glove. Its tubular steel exoskeleton rises to compliment the skyline from all directions.

Jacobs Field is, to borrow a phrase, a looker. Six levels, rising 120 feet from the main concourse to the top of its sunscreen, the ballpark is constructed of Atlantic green granite, Kasota stone, and Indiana limestone. Stonemasons from the Albert M. Higley Company labored like old world craftsmen to get it just right. Exposed structural steel is visible above the main concourse, a deft design touch not unrelated to the fact that Cleveland made its earliest fame and fortune as a steel town.

Yet there is a lightness about the design of Gateway. The bulk of both the ballpark and the arena has been minimized by lowering the ballfield 18 feet below street level and the arena's event floor 23 feet below the main concourse level. Baseball in this park is played under the sky, on green grass. The upper and lower seating areas have breezy concourses, terrific views of the city and its skyline, and good sight lines.

The ballpark's airy, open framework of steel, accented by brick, stone and glass, highlights the sinew of the structure. Above right, from Gateway Plaza, the Terrace Club Tower provides a dramatic backdrop for the Indians Box Office and Administration Building.

Above, *the steel buckles that have become the signature for the design of Jacobs Field. Inset right, cantilevered stairs above the main concourse boldly define the club seat and luxury suite walkways.*

PHOTOS. LEFT AND ABOVE: PAUL CHRISTOPHER © 1994

On and off the field, everything possible has been done to make the Gateway experience extraordinary.

Start with the natural grass field, where a drainage system enables the field to handle nine inches of rain, even if it pours down one hour before game time. The emerald-green sod that is the soul of the picture-perfect field was laid by the S.W. Franks Construction Company with fastidious care.

Or consider the seating — the deft work of the American Seating Company and Singleton Construction Company — which is angled 8 to 12 degrees to provide a better view of the field along

T*he displays and scoreboards throughout the ballpark, designed and manufactured by Daktronics, Inc., and Sony, use more than 72,000 incandescent lamps.*

And you won't miss the action even if you leave your seat. There are 451 twenty-one inch color TVs throughout the ballpark to keep you up-to-the-minute on the action.

Gateway: Blueprint Of The Future

the first and third base lines. And with wider aisles and more leg room, games are just plain more fun to watch.

The largest free-standing scoreboard in the country, installed by Forest City Erectors, Inc., is 220 feet wide by 70 feet high for a mammoth 15,000 plus square feet. It provides instant color replay clearly, even on the sunniest days. A smaller scoreboard keeps fans up-to-the-minute on scores from around the country.

A high-tech, state-of-the-art public address system that can be clearly heard is one of the many touches that makes the Jacobs Field experience unique. And the organ (a synthesizer, of course) adds to the old-fashioned fun-at-the-ballpark feeling.

Another touch is the diversity of concessions available at the ballpark. From gummi bears to deli sandwiches to fresh bakery, the choices are almost as interesting as the game.

Daktronics

Every time the Indians lineup flashes on the scoreboard at Jacobs Field, Daktronics and its state-of-the-art equipment put the team and its ballpark in outstanding company.

The company's display boards are lighting up in every state in America and 50 foreign countries. Jacobs Field joins Baltimore's Camden Yards, the Seattle Kingdome, the Minneapolis Metrodome, and the Ballpark at Arlington in providing baseball fans with Daktronics' visual thrills, color-animated characters, instant replays, and baseball scores from around the country.

Headquartered in Brookings, South Dakota, the 600-employee firm was formed by two South Dakota State University (SDSU) engineering professors — Al Kurtenbach, Ph.D., the company's CEO, and Duane Sanders, Ph.D., now dean of engineering at SDSU — who tired of seeing their graduates leave South Dakota for out-of-state jobs. Today, the company reports $35 million in sales of its scoreboards, message centers, voting systems and time-and-temperature boards.

In Cleveland, Daktronics provided the display unit and software to run the Jacobs Field scoreboard, while construction on the project was completed by local companies. The scoreboard operates on a software and statistical system that is second to none. All current baseball statistics are downloaded from Major League Baseball's computer system and all individual and team statistics are instantly updated on the scoreboard as the games progress. Statistics for the Indians are available at a moment's notice.

The Daktronics firm may be a long way from Cleveland, but it brings Indians fans closer to the action — not only at Gateway, but to the excitement that is major league baseball across America.

Indians **A**dministration Building Atrium, top; Clubhouse, above left; team weight room, above right; hydrotherapy spa, right.

Things noticeable and not-so-noticeable have made Jacobs Field a park for ball players as well as for fans. Elevated four feet, six inches above the ground, the bullpens have three mounds. Visiting relief pitchers warm up in right field; the Indians relief pitchers in center field.

The dugouts are something of an exception to baseball tradition. The home team dugout is almost always along the first-base line, but the Indians, to completely break with Municipal Stadium tradition, chose the dugout along the third-base line.

The new Indians clubhouse includes state-of-the-art weight and training rooms, a rehabilitation room and hydrotherapy spa. Hitters and hurlers can sharpen their skills in the four batting/pitching tunnels adjacent to the clubhouse.

Located along Ontario Avenue is the four-story Indians Administration Building. In addition to the team's administrative offices, the building is home to the Indians museum and gift shop.

The Administration Building, as seen from the Flats; the batting cage and pitching tunnel (right).

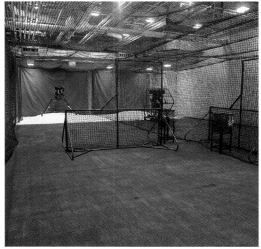

PHOTOS, LEFT AND ABOVE: PAUL CHRISTOPHER ©1994

the standard seats — and padded. The Club Lounge, which seats 450 people, is an exclusive fringe benefit for both club seat holders and luxury suite "owners".

The Terrace Club restaurant and bar, seating 619, is the largest single restaurant in Cleveland. With its curved staircase and handsome appointments, it is also one of the most attractive. Located along the third-base line, it offers nine levels of tiered seating. Seamless glass walls provide diners with a panoramic view of the field and the game.

Another inside-the-ballpark attraction is the picnic area in right-center field, between the scoreboard and Indians' bull pen. This area, with 117 tables, is available for corporate group and family outings.

While there isn't a bad seat to be found in the ballpark, premium seating is extra special. There are 2,000 club seats located along the first base line, between the lower and upper box seat sections. The seats are 22 inches wide — 3 inches wider than

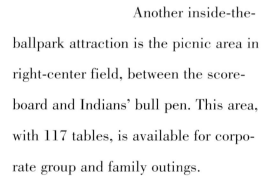

Cini•Little International

If you want to know how many hot dogs are needed for a baseball game at Jacobs Field, just ask Cini•Little.

In the hospitality and entertainment industry, Cini•Little, the largest firm of its kind, is known for having all the answers. The Chagrin Falls and Ft. Lauderdale offices, with their affiliate The Bigelow Companies, provided feasibility and marketing studies, and facilities designs for Jacobs Field food services.

For instance, they know that baseball fans only want to spend 45 to 60 seconds in line for a hotdog and drink, which means one outlet for each 250-300 seats. But Gateway wanted even better service, so Cini•Little increased the number of outlets at Jacobs Field to one for each 200 seats — so fans get even faster service.

The Club Lounge (facing page), for "owners" of club seats and luxury suites, is designed to fit beautifully into the Jacobs Field ambiance. Providing the visual focus of the setting are oil paintings immortalizing the sport of baseball, by Cleveland artist Jesse Rhinehart (to the right of his "bigger than life" painting). The Terrace Club restaurant and bar (right).

PHOTO, ABOVE: PAUL CHRISTOPHER © 1994

Stadium developers and entertainment facilities worldwide have turned to Cini•Little for food service design and development, including: The Georgia Dome; Olympic, and Joe Robbie Stadiums; Madison Square Garden; Chicago Bulls and Blackhawks arenas; Velladrome in Manchester, England; Universal Studios® and Disney® in Orlando, Florida; and Princess Cruise Lines®.

Headquartered in Rockville, Maryland, with offices world-wide, the Chagrin Falls office is a valuable civic partner for Cleveland, providing services for such economic development projects as Playhouse Square Foundation, Cleveland Playhouse, and downtown and Flats restaurant development.

So when you dine in Cleveland's finest restaurants, The Terrace Club, The Club Lounge, or visit any of the food service areas at Jacobs Field, you'll enjoy Cini•Little's attention to your convenience — and to the future of Cleveland.

Dugout Suites

Visitors Dugout

Indians Dugout

325'

Gateway: Blueprint Of The Future

There are 126 luxury suites in the park, each featuring a viewing area, bar, restroom, and television; 10 are field level dugout suites, just 58 feet behind home plate (above).

If you've never heard of "dugout suites", it's because they never existed until now. Tom Henneberry, of The Richard E. Jacobs Group, came up with the innovative concept. Spectators in these suites, located between the two dugouts, are closer to the catcher than the pitcher is.

Fans will want to bring their baseball gloves to Jacobs Field. Left and right field lines in the new ballpark each measure 325 feet. Deep center field measures 430 feet – sure to encourage the home-run hitter and put the fans on top of the game.

325'

Gateway Square

430'

Deep Center Field

From the beginning, Gateway was envisioned as a place that would be much more than "just a stadium."

It was meant to be a gathering place for all Clevelanders. Certainly, the complex would be the site of countless sports thrills — of come-from-behind victories and agonizing defeats. But, more than that, it would bring people from all corners of the region to stand side-by-side and mingle shoulder-to-shoulder for concerts, festivals, public celebrations and events of every conceivable kind. But how was this lofty ideal to be realized?

The first answer was to recognize the need for elastic public spaces; to incorporate such spaces into Gateway's very fabric; and to employ them as the link between the ballpark and the arena.

Gateway Plaza, the mall separating the ballpark from the arena, is no little patio. It's the size of two football fields.

Gateway has used design sleight-of-hand to make service vehicles disappear, hiding a 90,000 square-foot service garage under Gateway Plaza.

PHOTO: SKYVIEW PHOTOGRAPHY ©1994

Today, a variety of strategically-placed public parks and plazas, capable of accommodating people day or night, year-round, for events of all kinds, are an integral part of Gateway.

Gateway Plaza, sandwiched between Jacobs Field and the arena, is the largest. Designed to accommodate staging areas, lighting, sound systems, and all other necessities for mounting major dance, theatrical and musical presentations, its dimensions work as well for the lunch-time visitor as for crowds of 20,000 people. More than that, the Plaza is complemented year-round by a portion of Gateway's renowned public art collection.

*I*ndians Square draws curious pre-game fans. From reading the base of the more than one and one-half ton nine-foot bronze statue of Bob Feller, created by sculptor Gary Ross, to reading the paver stones, fans get into the spirit of Indians baseball at Jacobs Field. (For the record, the statue's granite base weighs 12 tons.)

A smaller plaza, Indians Square, located along East Ninth Street, features a bronze statue of Indians Hall-of-Fame pitcher Bob Feller. Paving stones, purchased by individuals and corporations, provided the funding for the statue, and create a carpet of names that highlight the public and private underpinnings of the Gateway project.

Two pedestrian bridges lead from the ballpark to the East Garage, an L-shaped, five-level structure built for 2,100 cars. A third pedestrian bridge leads from the arena to the East Garage, while yet another spans Huron Road from the arena, connecting with a 1,000-space North Parking Garage at the intersection of Huron Road and Ontario Avenue. There are 34,000 parking spaces within a 15-minute walk of the complex.

Other more intimate spaces are located at exits and entrances of Jacobs Field and the arena.

As the largest and most ambitious building project of our lifetimes, Gateway captured the imaginations of Clevelanders from the outset. What would it look like? How would it change the face of downtown Cleveland?

To explore these questions, interested local organizations (including the Committee for Public Art, Urban Design Center of Northeast Ohio and the Historic Gateway Neighborhood Development Corp.) joined forces to sponsor a series of public forums. The town hall meetings featured planning and architectural presentations, and fostered lively discussions about the hopes and concerns of citizens.

People hoped for a complex that would capture what is best and most worthwhile in the existing architecture and framework of their city. They wanted a place that would be people-friendly — for athletes and spectators, for common and uncommon folks alike — for all seasons.

PHOTO: PAUL CHRISTOPHER © 1994

An entirely new indoor public space (below) was created between Gateway and Tower City Center. A $14 million climate-controlled, glass and steel walkway links the two complexes.

Beginning at The Avenue, it spans the Tower City parking lot and rapid transit tracks, and becomes a 100-foot tunnel under Ontario Avenue leading to the arena. From there, it is only a short jaunt to Jacobs Field.

PHOTO: COURTESY URS CONSULTANTS

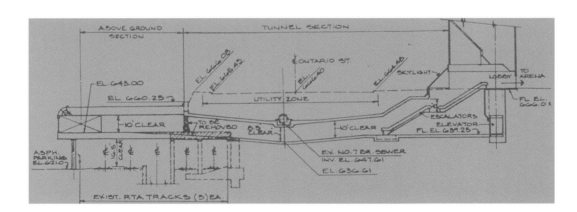

The industrial and commercial heritage of the city inspired Gateway's open-steel construction, influenced its public spaces, and provided the theme for its public art.

The catalyst for integrating public art into the Gateway environment was the Committee for Public Art (CPA) and Kathy Coakley, its executive director. In partnership with Gateway, the CPA set out to bring work of outstanding artists to Gateway's public parks and malls, in a unique outdoor collection – a collection that would touch on the functional, the humorous and the informative.

A jury of national and local art professionals culled submissions from 125 renowned artists, selecting five to develop special new work for the open-air, free-access spaces at Gateway.

The final works selected amounted to the largest installation of public art to be found in any major sports complex in America, represented by a fistful of national and local artists. They include Red Grooms, R.M. Fischer, Nancy Dwyer, Penny Rakoff and Angelica Pozo.

In a complex where the grace of the cleanly-executed double play is sure to be appreciated, public art adds a special grace of its own.

F*ive national and local artists were selected by a national jury to design works for Gateway— (left to right), R.M. Fischer, Nancy Dwyer, Angelica Pozo, Red Grooms, and Penny Rakoff.*

*A*ngelica Pozo and Penny Rakoff collaborated on the ceramic
bench which tells the history of the Gateway neighborhoods
and the markets that once flourished on the 28-acre site. Pozo,
a ceramic artist, and Rakoff, a photographer, brought their skills
together, ingeniously integrating colorful tiles, archival material
and archaeological artifacts unearthed during excavations on the
site prior to construction. Historic photos and ceramic representations
are juxtaposed and comprise the seating elements of this bench,
measuring 30 feet long, 7-1/2 feet wide, and 18 inches high.

R.M. Fischer's "Columns of Light" are monumental elements framing Gateway Plaza. The two soaring towers are stainless steel suffused with special lighting features and designs that are reminicient of the Flats and the industrial valley that provides the backdrop for Gateway. Functional as well, they provide ventilation and emergency egress from the underground service area.

The history of Cleveland is told from a unique civic perspective in the "Sculpto-pictorama" proposed by internally acclaimed artist Red Grooms. Approximately 30 feet tall, this contemporary monument features the glacier that created Lake Erie, landmark buildings and neighborhood scenes. These are a canvas for Cleveland's notable historical figures — from Jesse Owens to Margaret Bourke-White — who represent the rich human history of the city.

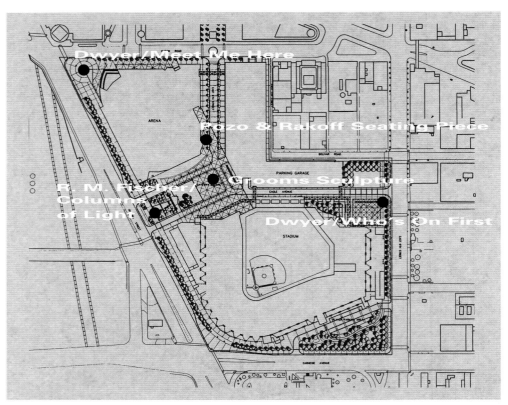

Carefully placed to blend with the architecture and the many diverse events hosted there, public art captures the spirit of Gateway in its open invitation to visit.

The attitude reflective of the Gateway experience is expressed in the two seating pieces by artist Nancy Dwyer that welcome people to Gateway: "Meet Me Here," located at the entrance to the arena, adjacent to the RTA tunnel and concourse; and "Who's On First?" inspired by Abbot and Costello's famous baseball routine, featured in Indians Square. Each letter in both is comprised of enormous separate letters of red granite, and provides an unusual opportunity to relax and enjoy Gateway.

"Who's on First?" *was the title and theme of the first non-baseball event held at Jacobs Field (upper right).*

With 1,100 people in attendance, over $400,000 was raised that night to benefit public art at Gateway, including the "sale" of the letters on the bench by the same name.

<small>PHOTO: PAUL CHRISTOPHER, ©1994.</small>

"The Committee for Public Art exists to bring the vision of artists to the community, and to advocate and facilitate public design on a human scale. Public art projects must be accessible to all, educate people about their common cultural heritage, and stimulate new thinking about the relationship of the arts to daily life."

— *Mission Statement*— *The Committee For Public Art*

Jacobs Field is indeed "more than just a stadium."

Everyone is invited to Jacobs Field. One innovative feature is Kid's Land – with concessions, novelties, and a play area, located in the right-field corner of the main concourse. The ballpark is also equipped with state-of-the-art conveniences for the disabled — visitors as well as Gateway employees. Rest rooms, concession stands, and luxury suites have been designed specifically for handicapped access. People in wheelchairs can sit in either a special section for wheelchairs or in the regular seating areas. There are special amplification devices for the deaf and Braille signage for the blind. The Cuyahoga County Commissioners Advisory Committee on Persons with Disabilities gave Gateway a four-star rating as one of the county's best-designed facilities.

PHOTOS: ABOVE AND BELOW: PAUL CHRISTOPHER, ©1994.

PHOTO: LEFT, AND FAR RIGHT, CHRISTOPHER RAMSEY ©1994.

What it all amounts to is a winner — a place for a winning attitude, a winning team, a winning season. Yet Jacobs Field is even more than these things, for what it represents is a new era in the history of Cleveland.

From Opening

Day 1994

forward,

Jacobs Field

is weaving

its own

memories,

its own legends,

its own history.

And what a

history it will be.

League Park—1893-1947

Gateway: Blueprint Of The Future

Cleveland Municipal Stadium—1932-1993

Gateway: Blueprint Of The Future

J acobs Field at Gateway—1994

Blueprint

of the Future

This 21st century sports complex is profoundly impacting down- town Cleveland in a variety of ways; immediate and long term, physically and economically, culturally and aesthetically, changing forever the way Clevelanders feel about their city.

PHOTO: ©1994 PAUL CHRISTOPHER

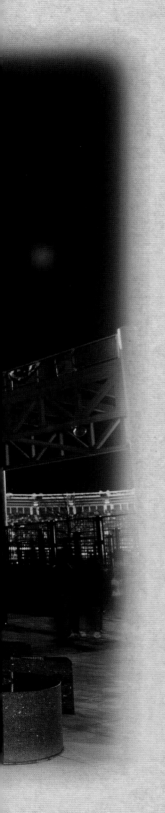

There is the immediate effect Gateway has as the newest super sports-complex in the country. Here's what it amounts to: a ballpark and arena, along with two parking garages for 3,200 cars, and 8.5 acres of public open space, on 28 acres of land in downtown Cleveland.

Planned to accommodate 81 major league baseball games and 41 NBA basketball games annually, the multi-purpose sports complex also will host 41 ice hockey and six arena football games, other sports events, concerts, family entertainment, and convention events. In total, there will be more than 250 activities each year, attracting some five million visitors.

But that is only part of the Gateway story. Its short-term impact on the pocketbooks of workers and businesses was impressive and immediate. By the end of 1992,

Gateway had created nearly 700 jobs. Almost $100 million had gone to area businesses for goods and services. By the time it was completed, more than 4,000 people had been employed in the construction of Gateway.

Committed to providing business opportunities to minorities and females, Gateway established a two-tiered affirmative action policy. Goals of 22.6 percent minority participation and 6.9 percent female participation for building trades people working on the Gateway site were met and, in some instances, exceeded. Goals of awarding 30 percent of construction project contracts to Minority Business Enterprise and 10 percent to Female Business Enterprise were established for all prime contractors.

Another impact of Gateway is the way in which it has influenced its own neighborhood. At the grass-roots level, local merchants in Cleveland's oldest shopping area, East 4th Street and Prospect Avenue, began a coordinated effort to revitalize the district. It was once home of the Opera House and some of the most elegant shops in Cleveland.

In January of 1991, the Historic Gateway Neighborhood (HGN), formerly the East 4th/Prospect Avenue Local Development Corporation, began looking for ways to revitalize the district. An early success came with the Storefront Renovation Program, run by the City of Cleveland. The program offered property owners rebates or low interest loans and free restoration design assistance. The first project was at the Sincere Building on East 4th Street, and included a new marble exterior, new signage, a rebuilt marquee, and the repair of the building's terra cotta.

In October of 1991, another big step was taken with the hiring of the HGN's first full-time managing director. Fittingly enough, that person was Peter Holmes, a former newspaper man and president of the National Press Club, who happens to be the son of the late Allen Holmes.

Peter Holmes says his father's hopes for Gateway had a great deal more to do with Cleveland's economic future than with its baseball future. "He wanted this first and foremost as an economic development project. He was no great fan of baseball. Football was his sport."

"There's a terrific opportunity here," says Holmes, "and it's a question of getting merchants to understand the opportunity and take advantage of it."

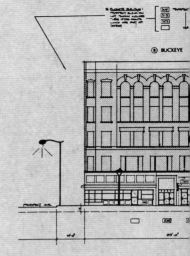

AStreetscape Plan, half underwritten by Gateway, was a catalyst for the revitalization of roadways and streetscapes in the neighborhood. The HGN has promoted Common Area Programs (CAPs), which deal with advertising, parking, security, and cleanliness.

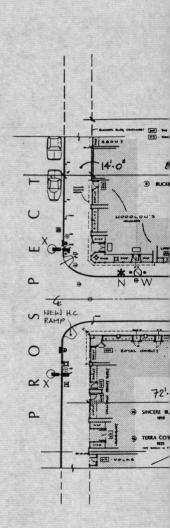

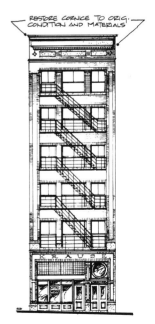

UPPER FACADE

REMODELED OR RESTORED STOREFRONTS MUST BE DESIGNED SO THAT THEY ARE COMPATIBLE IN PROPORTION/MATERIALS TO THE UPPER BUILDING FACADE.

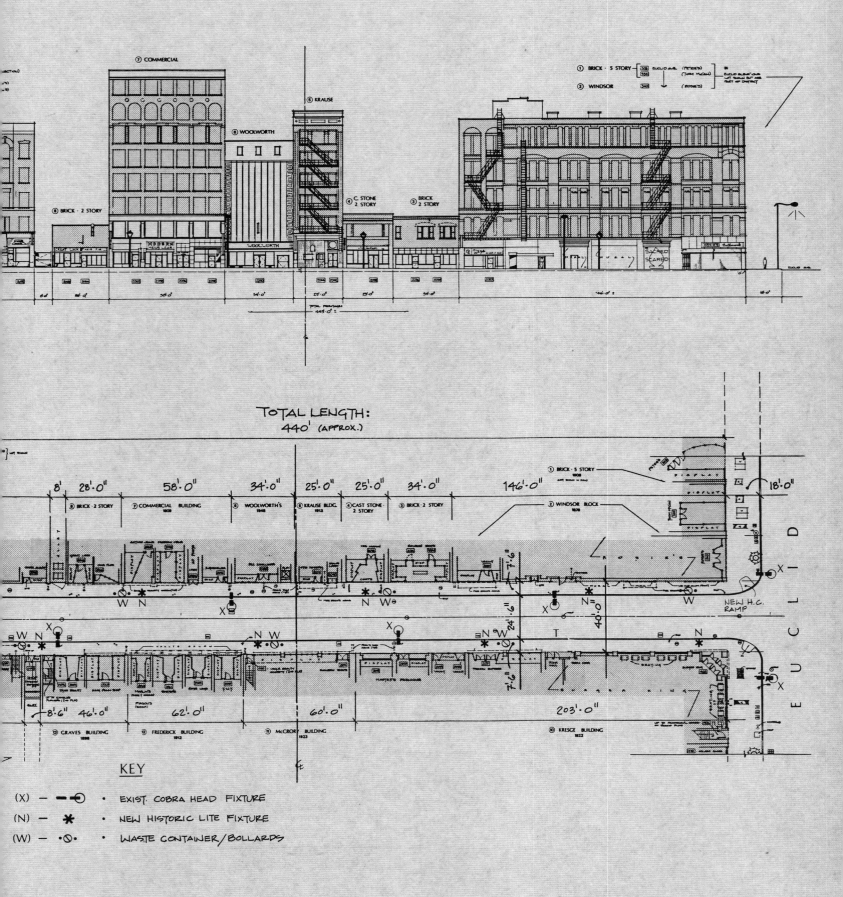

① BRICK · 5 STORY
② WINDSOR

⑦ COMMERCIAL
⑤ KRAUSE
⑥ WOOLWORTH
④ C. STONE 2 STORY
③ BRICK 2 STORY
⑧ BRICK · 2 STORY

TOTAL LENGTH:
440' (APPROX.)

8' · 28'·0" · 58'·0" · 34'·0" · 25'·0" · 25'·0" · 34'·0" · 146'·0" · 18'·0"

⑧ BRICK · 2 STORY
⑦ COMMERCIAL BUILDING 1908
⑥ WOOLWORTH'S
⑤ KRAUSE BLDG. 1913
④ CAST STONE 2 STORY
③ BRICK · 2 STORY

① BRICK · 5 STORY 1908
② WINDSOR BLOCK 1878

NEW H.C. RAMP

8'·6" 46'·0" · 62'·0" · 60'·0" · 203'·0"

⑨ GRAVES BUILDING 1898
⑦ FREDERICK BUILDING 1912
⑪ McCRORY BUILDING 1923
⑩ KRESGE BUILDING 1922

E U C L I D

KEY

(X) — —● · EXIST. COBRA HEAD FIXTURE

(N) — ✳ · NEW HISTORIC LITE FIXTURE

(W) — ·⊘· · WASTE CONTAINER/BOLLARDS

GRAPHICS: COURTESY GAEDE SERNE ARCHITECTS INC.

The opportunities have prompted HGN and various other organizations, including the Indians, Cavaliers, and Gateway, to become members of the Downtown Development Coordinators, Inc. (DDC). Officially founded in March of 1993, the DDC serves as a coordinator of public and private development initiatives in the area between Public Square and Playhouse Square, and north of Carnegie Avenue and south of Euclid Avenue.

The man selected to serve as the DDC chairman was dividing his time between his home in Cleveland and the one he owns near Fort Lauderdale overlooking the 10th tee of a golf course. "I'm down in Florida, I'm retired, enjoying life. They drafted me," laughs former U.S. Judge Alvin I. "Buddy" Krenzler.

"They" included Albert Ratner of Forest City Enterprises and Cleveland Mayor Michael White. The DDC was an outgrowth of a cooperative effort between the mayor and Ratner to get those individuals with a stake in downtown Cleveland to join in making certain the policies and goals established for the growth of downtown were implemented.

"We decided we'd be an action group, not a conversation group," says Judge Krenzler. To that end, the DDC focused on both short- and long-term projects throughout downtown Cleveland. These ranged from improved downtown lighting to the consideration of the future of the Cleveland Convention Center and the need for more housing downtown. But because of the Gateway project, the Historic Gateway Neighborhood became the initial focus of the DDC.

One of the DDC's first major efforts was to repair the basements owned by merchants and other businesses along Prospect Avenue and elsewhere in the Gateway impact area. Though privately owned, the basements are part of the public right-of-way – sidewalks are their roofs. Until the basements were repaired, streets in the area could not be improved. Eight million dollars in federal and state funds for street repair work sat idle. Working with city officials, the DDC recommended that the basements' owners be assessed for basement repairs. Appropriate legislation was passed in Cleveland City Council, which resulted in the basements being repaired in short order.

"We should have videotaped that and showed it in civics classes," says Judge Krenzler. The

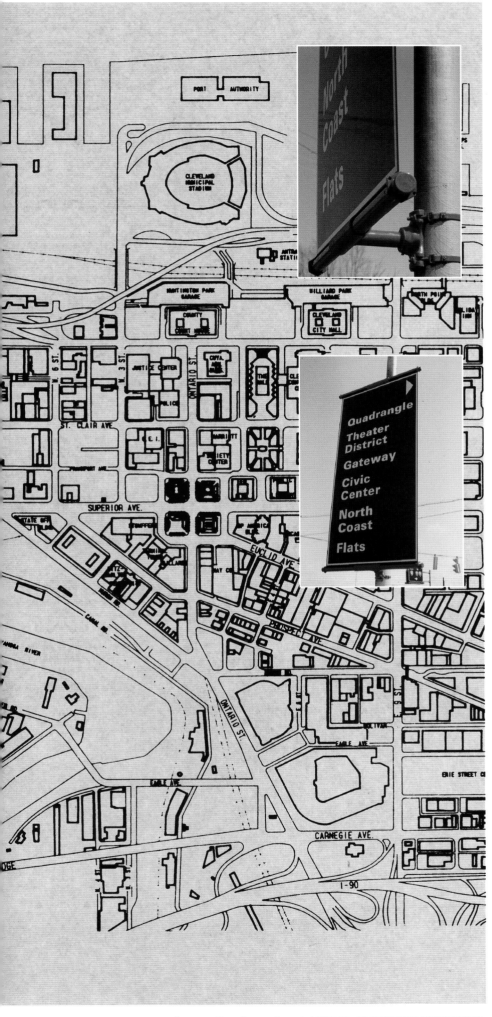

GRAPHIC AND PHOTOS COURTESY THOMPSON & WOOD INC., AND THE DOWNTOWN DEVELOPMENT CORP.

repairs were followed by the widening of sidewalks, the resurfacing of the streets, the replacement of streetlights with pedestrian lighting, landscaping, and the renovation of storefronts on Prospect and East 4th Street. Unsightly scissors-type security gates were discouraged.

On a broader scale, the DDC took on projects that impacted all of downtown Cleveland. Among them were downtown signage, safety, housing, and retail programs.

A steering committee of the DDC developed a safety agenda that included private and public security, made recommendations to encourage the construction of 10,000 new housing units in downtown areas, as well as for new retail businesses needed to serve residents of the units.

It also was instrumental in proposing what could become one of the most creative approaches to re-energizing downtown Cleveland: a

Initiated by Downtown Development Corporation and designed by Thompson & Wood, Inc., an innovative signage and wayfinding program has established Cleveland as the first major city with plans for a complete downtown signage project.

Downtown Development Authority. Such an Authority requires state and local legislation. "A Downtown Development Authority can do what the city does but sometimes can't afford to do, or do what the city doesn't do," says Krenzler. An Authority Board of Trustees would make policy and adopt resolutions providing for various services, which would be paid for by the owners of property in the downtown development area.

Gateway's impact resulted in a coalition of downtown neighborhoods, organizations, merchants, and public and private interests unlike anything the town had ever seen before.

That impact was felt by every downtown neighborhood, every merchant who works there, and every citizen who lives or visits there. It was the right project at the right time in the life of the city. Like the pinch hitter who wins a tie ball game by drilling one over the fence in the bottom of the ninth, or the shooting guard who hits the winning three-pointer at the buzzer, Gateway delivered what the city needed, when it was needed.

In every respect, Gateway is the tether tying all the economic hopes and dreams of downtown Cleveland together. Before the ballpark opened, 300 new jobs were created in the immediate neighborhood with the opening of seven new restaurants. A complete crescent of entertainment, recreational and leisure-time development has emerged. It includes a vast sweep of projects, from the Rock and Roll Hall of Fame and Museum to Playhouse Square.

Gateway: Blueprint Of The Future

The Cleveland Lumberjacks

The rich North Coast ice hockey tradition is alive and well, thanks to the "Jacks".

Ice hockey has been a part of Cleveland's sports scene since the "Indians", its first professional hockey team, won the International Hockey League (IHL) championship in its first year of play in 1929.

In 1934, Al Sutphin, Cleveland businessman and sports promoter, bought the team and renamed it the "Falcons". A visionary, Sutphin watched his dream come true as the Cleveland Arena, located at East 37th Street and Euclid Avenue, opened in 1937, the same year the Falcons joined the American Hockey League and changed their name to the "Barons".

Cleveland fans thrilled as the team skated to eight Calder Cup championships in 27 years. Nick Mileti sold the team in 1964, then four years later formed the "Crusaders" who took to the ice for another slapshot-filled decade.

It took 20 years, the city's love for the sport, and the promise of Gateway's new downtown arena to lure Larry Gordon and his "Zephyrs" to Cleveland in 1992. Two years later, Gordon purchased the Muskegon team and christened them the "Lumberjacks". Under his leadership, the team enjoyed success and a reputation as a top minor league affiliate for the Pittsburgh Penguins. Six former players went on to play crucial roles in the Penguins' back-to-back Stanley Cup victories in the 1989-90 and 1990-91 seasons.

Gordon, a strong believer in community service, is a trustee of Shoes for Kids. His team donates proceeds from ticket sales and player jersey raffles to charity, and the players and staff support United Way, Harvest for Hunger, Caring Sharing Charities, Toys for Tots, and the American Red Cross. They also are regular visitors at Rainbow Babies and Children's Hospital and area schools.

Larry Gordon knows a winner when he sees one. With the start of the 1994-95 season at Gateway, a downtown tradition of professional ice hockey excitement will be rekindled on the North Coast. With the Lumberjacks, Cleveland is a winner.

Glittering brightly within this crescent are such mega-projects as the $268-million Tower City Center retail-entertainment complex, the Galleria, the Flats entertainment district, the Warehouse District, and North Coast Harbor. And Gateway, expected to generate a billion dollars in economic development by the end of the century, was the last critical stone needed for building the future prosperity and well-being of downtown Cleveland.

PHOTOS:
©1994
MORT
TUCKER

Gateway is perfectly positioned to stimulate growth and development for all of downtown. The Avenue (left) connects directly to Gateway via the RTA concourse and tunnel; the Flats (above) are just a short walk away for dining before and after events at Gateway; and the Galleria (top) is only minutes due north on East Ninth Street.

The Cleveland Thunderbolts

What began as a concept scribbled on an envelope seven years ago has now established itself as a force to be reckoned with in the professional sports community: arena football.

Fans across the country are lining up in record numbers to experience the thrill of a game that combines the strategy of football, the fast-paced action of basketball, and the hard-hitting drive of hockey—with a healthy dose of rock and roll and a few fireworks thrown in for good measure. Owner John Kuzek, who brought the fledgling Thunderbolts to Cleveland in 1992, recognized the appeal the sport would have. Since then, a growing number of dedicated fans call the Thunderbolts their number-one hometown team.

Unlike conventional football, arena football is played indoors, on padded artificial turf to protect the players from injury. The field is 50 yards long and 28 yards wide, has eight-yard end zones, with 30-by-32-foot rebound nets on each side of the goal posts. A four-foot-high padded wall surrounds the field, preventing players from running out of bounds to avoid a tackle, so passing dominates the action. A ball caught off rebound nets or bounces off padded walls is live.

A team consists of eight players: two down linemen, a fullback, a tight end, three wide receivers, and a quarterback. Everyone plays both offense and defense except the kicker, the quarterback, and the quarterback's replacement on defense. Only one linebacker may blitz and only one substitution can be made per quarter.

The most fundamental difference between arena and regular football is that the clock never stops as long as the ball is in play, much like soccer, except for one time-out in the final minute of each half. And when a fan catches a ball, it becomes a souvenir. Hard-driving rock music after each play—hence the nickname "rock-and-roll football" – and blasts of fireworks that punctuate the game keep excitement at a fever pitch. When the Thunderbolts move to their new home in Gateway's arena in the summer of 1995, win or lose, fans will come away feeling as exhilarated as the players.

The Thunderbolts are fast becoming one of the city's biggest boosters and community partners. The "Be Like Y'ikes Get High on Life" campaign, named after the purple, people-loving mascot, has reached hundreds of school children about the importance of staying drug- and alcohol-free. The team has also participated in a number of local charitable and civic activities, and are active members of the Convention & Visitors Bureau and the Greater Cleveland Growth Association.

A fast-paced team in a fast-paced sport, the Cleveland Thunderbolts are key players in a city where growth is setting its own record.

Spectacular as it is, Gateway is no pyramid, built simply to admire but returning nothing on its investment. As the largest public-works project in America in the early 1990s, Gateway is a catalyst for people and organizations with vested interests in the urban heart of Cleveland, bringing them together to share ideas, goals, and actions.

And as much as Gateway is the capstone of a revitalized Cleveland, even more, it is the cornerstone for the building of a new Cleveland.

There are different kinds of greatness, and Gateway epitomizes Cleveland's aspirations. Built on a foundation of blast furnaces and machine manufacturing, Cleveland was one of many American cities that had to cope with an economy swept by forces of change. Its future lies not only in steel mills and foundries, but in the no less critical industries of service, leisure, and tourism.

Hammered and bolted and riveted together like some great galactic ship moored majestically on a field of dreams, Gateway is poised to take Cleveland into the future. For many, it represents Cleveland's opportunity to reclaim its place as one of America's foremost cities. "One of the things I was taught is that if a city was

PHOTOS: ABOVE, JENNY JONES ©1994, BELOW, MORT TUCKER ©1994.

once great, it can be great again," says Albert Ratner.

Gateway's vitality is already spilling into adjoining streets and neighborhoods. The new economic energy is generating construction of apartments, retail stores and parking garages, and is projected to bring a population of 20,000 people to the rein-vigorated, redeveloped, re-energized downtown.

Gateway proved that cooperation between business, civic and political leaders, could and did accomplish what other cities, and even Cleveland, had written off as impossible.

It is this lesson of achievement that rightfully positions Gateway as the Blueprint of the Future.

A.G. Mauro Company, 310 Alpha Dr.

   Pittsburgh, PA, 15238, 412-782-6600

AGA Gas & Welding, 6470 SOM Center Rd.

   Solon, OH, 44139, 216-349-1100

Able Contracting Group, 33100 Lakeland Blvd.

   Eastlake, OH, 44095, 216-951-0880

Access Elevator Co., 6240 Mayfield Rd.

   Cleveland, OH, 44124, 216-442-3514

Acme Arsena Co., Inc., 18440 Cranwood Pkwy.

   Warrensville Hts., OH, 44128, 216-581-7200

Action Door, 10779 Brookpark Rd.

   Cleveland, OH, 44130, 216-267-1450

Advantage/Martien Elect, 5030 Advantage Blvd.

   Toledo, OH, 43612, 419-881-3131

Akron Block & Brick Co., 3225 Mogadore Rd.

   Akron, OH, 44312, 216-628-2603

Albert Herman Draperies, 2035 Hamilton Ave.

   Cleveland, OH, 44114, 216-348-1500

ALL ERECTION & CRANE RENTAL, INC.

   7809 OLD ROCKSIDE RD., CLEVELAND, OH 44131

   216-524-6550

Allega Cement Co., 5585 Canal Rd.

   Valley View, OH, 44125, 216-447-0814

American Bridge Co., 3 Gateway Ctr.

   Pittsburgh, PA, 15222, 412-562-4474

American International Const, 60 Lincoln Ave.

   Berea, OH, 44017, 216-243-5535

American Seating Co., 901 Broadway Ave., NW.

   Grand Rapids, MI, 49504, 616-732-6655

Amsysco Inc., 740 Racquet Club Dr.

   Addison, IL, 60101, 708-628-6969

Architectural Products Co., 4641 Spring Rd.

   Brooklyn Hts., OH, 44131, 216-459-0500

Arnold Trucking/R & R, 4228 East 178th St.

   Cleveland, OH, 44128, 216-751-6948

Arrow Fabricating, 7300 Bessemer Ave.

   Cleveland, OH, 44127, 216-641-0490

Automatic Mechanical, 5141 Dickens Dr.

   Cleveland, OH, 44143, 216-752-3129

Automatic Sprinkler Corp., 10668 Progress Dr.

   Strongsville, OH, 44136, 216-238-9330

B-Par, Inc., P O Box 927,

   Willoughby, OH, 44094, 216-942-2242

Bean & Bennett Enterprise, 21651 Lakeshore Blvd.

   Euclid, OH, 44132, 216-289-2393

Bertin, D.A., Company, 1305 Brookpark Rd.

   Cleveland, OH, 44109, 216-661-5650

Bradley Construction Co., 13715 Kinsman Rd.

   Cleveland, OH, 44120, 216-283-6697

Brunswick Welding, 1239 Saxon Dr.

   Brunswick, OH, 44212, 216-225-4057

Burghardt Metal Fabricating, 1638 McCheshey Rd.

   Akron, OH, 44306, 216-794-1830

Burkshire Construction, 4213 Biddulph Rd.

   Cleveland, OH, 44109, 216-398-0908

CA Commercial Sheetmetal, 20710 Miles Pkwy.

   Cleveland, OH, 44128, 216-662-2882

Cabinet En-Counters, Inc., 6265 Mayfield Rd.

   Mayfield Hts., OH, 44124, 216-442-8604

Calabrese Cement, 700 East 165th St.

   Cleveland, OH, 44110, 216-481-7711

CALFEE HALTER & GRISWOLD

   McDONALD INVESTMENT CTR., CLEVELAND, OH 44114

   216-622-8200

Carron Asphalt Paving Co., 7615 Bond St.

   Solon, OH, 44139, 216-439-6464

Central Concrete Co., 900 Clark Ave.

   Cleveland, OH, 44113, 216-771-5200

Central Electric Supply, 23209 Miles Rd.

   Cleveland, OH, 44128, 216-581-4000

Charles Phipps Co.,7700 Harvard Ave.

   Cleveland, OH, 44105, 216-641-2150

Chiancone Landscape, P.O.Box 21550

   South Euclid, OH, 44121, 216-381-8835

Gateway: Blueprint Of The Future

Choice Construction Co., 3494 Lee Rd.
Cleveland, OH, 44120, 216-991-0003

Cirullo Steel Erectors, 686 South Munroe Rd.
Tallmadge, OH, 44278, 216-633-2512

Classic Marble Co., 8219 Almira Ave.
Cleveland, OH, 44102, 216-961-1678

Cleveland Architech H.W., 10576 Broadview Rd.
Cleveland, OH, 44147, 216-526-2710

Cleveland Cement Contractors, Inc., 4823 Van Epps
Rd., Cleveland, OH, 44131, 216-741-3954

CLEVELAND ELECTRIC ILLUMINATING CO.
55 Public Sq., Cleveland, OH 44103
216-622-9800

CLEVELAND PLUMBING CONTRACTORS
ASSOCIATION
981 Keynote Circle #30
Cleveland, OH 44131, 216-459-0770
Representing more than 105 member companies
throughout Northeast Ohio, the Cleveland
Plumbing Contractors Association (CPCA) serves
management at union-affiliated plumbing-contrac-
tor companies. CPCA represented all the plumbing
contractors on the Gateway site, and provides its
members with a number of trade services, including education and training, labor relations, and
code assistance.

CINI•LITTLE, INTERNATIONAL, INC.
139 Bell St., Chagrin Falls, OH 44022
216-247-4830

Coast Security Corp., 871 Ethan Allen Hgwy.
Ridgefield, CT, 06877, 216-431-0838

ColeJon Corporation, 13836 Union Ave.
Cleveland, OH, 44120, 216-991-2022

Collinwood Shale & Brick, 12400 Broadway Ave.
Cleveland, OH, 44125, 216-587-2700

Commercial Insulation Inc., 23200 Chagrin Blvd.
Beachwood, OH, 44122, 216-292-8189

Commercial Siding Co., 8059 Crile Rd.
Painesville, OH, 44077, 216-352-7800

Commsteel, Inc., 900 East 69th St.
Cleveland, OH, 44103, 216-881-4600

Complete Metal Contracting, 2530 Superior Ave.
Cleveland, OH, 44114, 216-522-0505

Concrete Cut'g & Break'g, 443 Jefferson St.
Grand Rapids, MI, 49503, 616-451-2886

Conservation of Energy, 711 Harvard Ave.
Cuyahoga Hts., OH, 44105, 216-271-3363

Construction Specialties, P.O.Box 380
Muncy, PA, 17756, 717-546-5941

Cook Paving & Construction, 5545 Canal Rd.
Cleveland, OH, 44125, 216-641-0551

Coon Caulking & Sealants, P. O. Box 259
Ravenna, OH, 44641, 216-875-2100

Courion Industries Inc., 3044 Lambdin Ave.
St. Louis, MO, 63115, 800-533-5760

Crest Masonry Inc., 320 Alpha Pk.
Highland Heights, OH, 44143, 216-461-6101

Cuyahoga Concrete Co., 2100 Central Furnace Ct.
Cleveland, OH, 44115, 216-771-0010

Cuyahoga Supply & Tool, 5340 Perkins Rd.
Cleveland, OH, 44146, 216-439-9393

Cuyahoga Valley Erectors, 7769 Crestwood Rd.
Northfield, OH, 44067, 216-478-0957

D & M Express, P. O. Box 2019
Akron, OH, 44309, 216-482-9208

D.W. Ross Insulation, Inc., 3190 West 63rd St.

    Cleveland, OH, 44102, 216-631-8080

DAKTRONICS INC.

331 32ND AVE.,BROOKINGS, SD, 57006,

800-843-5843

Day Electric Co., 7471 Tyler Blvd.

    Mentor, OH, 44060 216-946-3002

Dayton Showcase Co., 2601 West Dorothy Ln.

    Dayton, OH, 45439, 800-837-0321

Dellovade, Inc., A. C., 108 Cavasina Dr.

    Canonsburg, PA, 15317, 412-873-8190

Dependable Painting Co., 4403 Superior Ave.

    Cleveland, OH, 44103, 216-431-4470

Diamond Interiors, 300 Burton St.

    Fairport Harbor, OH, 44077, 216-354-6484

Doan Electric, 1807 East 22nd St.

    Cleveland, OH, 44114, 216-621-1467

Domestic Marble & Stone, 41 East 42nd St.

    New York, NY, 10017, 212-557-1980

Dominic Farinacci, 8022 Chardon Rd.

    Kirtland, OH, 44094, 216-946-1117

DONLEY'S, INC.

5430 WARNER RD.

CLEVELAND, OH, 44125, 216-524-6800

Dover Elevator Co., 1414 East Schaaf Rd.

    Cleveland, OH, 44131, 216-749-7883

Duct Fabricators, 883 Addison Rd.

    Cleveland, OH, 44103, 216-391-2400

Duvinage Corp., P.O. Box 828

    Hagerstown, MD, 21741, 301-733-8255

EL-O Electric Co., 812 Huron Rd., Suite 670

    Cleveland, OH, 44115, 216-781-6601

EPI OF CLEVELAND, INC.

1600 WEST MILL RD., PENINSULA, OH 44264

216-468-2872

EPI of Cleveland, Inc. is a miscellaneous metal
fabricator of stairs, railings and other special materials and items, in business for more than 32 years
serving the Greater Cleveland market. EPI was the
prime contractor on the Gateway ballpark,
installing 36,000 linear feet of handrail and 76
entrance gates.

Educational Equipment Co., 18233 S. Miles Rd.

    Cleveland, OH, 44128, 216-662-3150

Edward Simon & Co., 5933 Broad St.

    Pittsburgh, PA, 15206, 800-541-6595

Edwards-Sorma Corp., 1419 East 40th St.

    Cleveland, OH, 44103, 216-431-1662

Ellerbe Beckett, Inc., 605 West 47th St.

    Kansas, MO, 64112, 816-561-4443

Erectors, Inc., 20 East North St.

    Akron, OH, 44304, 216-762-6461

Finley Fabricators, Inc., 1000 Addison Rd.

    Cleveland, OH, 44103, 216-881-5544

Flooring Specialties, 23940 Miles Rd.

    Warrensville Hts., OH, 44128, 216-662-7290

Flooring Specialty Co., 23940 Miles Rd.

    Cleveland, OH, 44129, 216-662-7290

Forest City Erectors Inc., 8300 Boyle Pkwy.

    Twinsburg, OH, 44087, 216-425-7185

Foti Construction Co., 2501 West Third St.

    Cleveland, OH, 44113, 216-621-0925

Fox Fire Protection Co., 15300 Pearl Rd.

    Strongsville, OH, 44136, 216-238-5543

Franklin Roofing, Inc., 7757 Auburn Rd.

    Painesville, OH, 44077, 216-352-6777

Functional Building Supply, 4472 Cranwood Pkwy.

    Cleveland, OH, 44113, 216-587-4666

GQ Drywall Company, 1164 Lloyd Rd.

    Wickliffe, OH, 44092, 216-585-3580

GIAMBRONE MASONRY, INC.

22151 AURORA RD.

BEDFORD HEIGHTS, OH 44146

216-475-0338

Giambrone Masonry, Inc. is a brick and stone contractor that has earned an outstanding reputation
during its 17-year history in masonry construction.

Gilbert Co., 2500 Morrison Rd.

    Dexter, MI, 48130, 313-426-3433

GIORGI INTERIOR SYSTEMS, INC.

5075 TAYLOR RD., BEDFORD HEIGHTS

OH 44128, 216-663-3737

Giorgi Interior Systems, Inc., a full-service contractor with more than 24 years of success in the construction industry, worked as a carpentry subcontractor for the Indians Administration Building,
installing metal framing, acoustical ceilings, plaster
and drywall.

Gleeson Construction, 178 Solon Rd.

    Chagrin Falls, OH, 44022, 216-247-8775

Goodall-Grivas. Inc., 17320 West Eight Mile Rd.
Southfield, MI, 48075, 313-569-0300

Gorman-Lavelle Corp., 3459 East 52nd Pl.
Cleveland, OH, 44114, 216-641-4600

Granger Trucking Co., 8001 Old Granger Rd.
Cleveland, OH, 44125, 216-641-5015

Gratton Building Specials, 7575 Tyler Blvd.
Mentor, OH, 44060, 216-951-7885

Great Lakes Hotel Supply, 1961 Grand River Ave.
Detroit, MI, 48226, 313-962-9176

Griffin Dewatering Corp., 3450 Calumet Ave.
Hammond, IN, 46320, 219-931-1662

Grinnell Fire Protection, 1294 East 55th St.
Cleveland, OH, 44103, 216-431-5700

Gypsum Construction, 7539 Fern Dr.
Mentor, OH, 44060, 216-257-3930

H. C. Painting Co., Inc, 3617 Lee Rd.
Shaker Heights, OH, 44120, 216-751-4844

H-MAK, Inc., Three Beta Dr.
Pittsburgh, PA, 15238, 412-826-8088

Hammond Mechanical, Inc., P. O. Box 17048
Euclid, OH, 44117, 216-692-2112

Harmon Glass & Contract, 850 South Marietta St.
South Bend, IN, 46601, 219-233-3511

Harrington Electric Co., 3800 Perkins Ave.
Cleveland, OH, 44114, 216-361-5101

Harsh Engineering Services, 4935 S. Prospect St.
Ravenna, OH, 44266, 216-297-0301

Hastings Pavement Co., 30 Commercial St.
Freeport, NY, 11520

Haw Associates, S M, 9501 Allen Dr.
Cleveland, OH, 44125, 216-447-0117

Hayes Construction Co., 386 Eddy Rd.
Cleveland, OH, 44108, 216-851-8050

Higley, Albert M., Co., 2926 Chester Ave.
Cleveland, OH, 44114, 216-861-2050

Hirsch Electric Co., 5060 Corbin Dr.
Bedford Hts., OH, 44128, 216-662-6800

HUBER, HUNT & NICHOLS
P. O. Box 126, Indianapolis, IN 46206
317-241-6301

Hume Sales Company, 43 Alpha Park Dr.
Cleveland, OH, 44143, 216-449-0950

IEA Electric Corp., 16912 Miles Rd.
Cleveland, OH, 44128, 216-283-1232

INDEPENDENCE EXCAVATING
5720 Schaaf Rd., Independence, OH 44131
216-423-1700

Indiana Limestone Co., 405 North I St.
Bedford, IN, 47421, 812-275-3341

Industrial First, 16400 Miles Ave.
Cleveland, OH, 44128, 216-991-8600

Insulation Specialty, 1650 Crossings Pkwy.
Westlake, OH, 44145, 216-892-9250

Interior Steel Equip. Co., 2352 East 69th St.
Cleveland, OH, 44104, 216-881-0100

INTERNATIONAL UNION OF OPERATING
ENGINEERS , LOCAL UNION NO. 18
3515 Prospect Ave., Cleveland, OH 44115
216-432-3131

International Union of Operating Engineers Local Union No. 18 represents and services approximately 13,000 members through its six district and headquarters offices in Ohio, covering: building, highway, and railroad construction; sewer work reclamation; work on the Great Lakes; new equipment dealer shops (mechanics); county employees; and power and nuclear plants. On the Gateway project, they provided more than 70 skilled operators to 16 contractors, for operating 64 pieces of heavy equipment and machinery.

Interstate Safety & Services, Co., 3566 E. 55th St.
Cleveland, OH, 44105, 216-641-6776

Ironcraft, Inc., 3319 East 80th St.
Cleveland, OH, 44127, 216-341-1419

J-L Fire Equipment Co., P O Box 35403
Cleveland, OH, 44135, 216-252-3851

JMB Erection, Inc., 8365 Lucerne Dr.
Bainbridge, OH, 44023

Jay's Boom Trucking, 19110 Hathaway Ln.
Cleveland, OH, 44122, 216-752-0720

Jeffery Bogart Architechts, 2217 East 9th St.
Cleveland, OH, 44115, 216-696-0700

Judd Interior Contractors, Inc., 7290 Farhills Rd.
Concord, OH, 44077, 216-352-4435

Kapton Caulking Co., 6500 Harris Rd.
Cleveland, OH, 44147, 216-526-0670

Kelley Steel Erection, Inc., 7220 Division St.
Bedford, OH , 44146, 216-741-1130

Kilroy Structural Steel Co., 8500 Union Ave.

    Cleveland, OH, 44105, 216-883-3000

Kinsdale Construction, 15712 Miles Ave.

    Cleveland, OH, 44128, 216-752-8878

Lake Erie Electric, 25730 First St.

    Westlake, OH, 44145, 216-835-5565

Lakeside Blueprint Co., 4507 Lorain Ave.

    Cleveland, OH, 44102, 216-281-1234

Lakewood Architectural, 2293 Winfield Ave.

    Rocky River, OH, 44116, 216-333-8830

Landis & Gyr Powers, Inc., 7700 Hub Pkwy.

    Valley View, OH, 44125, 216-447-1343

Leader Electric Supply Co., 4300 Superior Ave.

    Cleveland, OH, 44103, 216-361-4540

M & R Mechanical, 11512 Superior Ave.

    Cleveland, OH, 44106, 216-421-0242

Mankato-Kasota Stone, 818 North Willow St.

    Mankato, MN, 56002, 507-625-2746

Marous Bros. Construction, 38046 Second St.

    Willoughby, OH, 44094, 216-951-3904

Martin Surfacing & Deck, P.O. Box 1289

    Hunt Valley, MD, 21030, 800-673-2402

M. Zunt, Inc., 600 A Terminal Tower

    Cleveland, OH, 44113, 216-696-8994

Mays Trucking Co., 3703 East 103rd St.

    Cleveland, OH, 44104, 216-341-6797

McGarry and Sons, 1200 East 49th St.

    Cleveland, OH, 44114, 216-361-1271

MECHANICAL CONTRACTORS
ASSOCIATION, INC.

981 Keynote Circle #30

Cleveland, OH 44131

216-459-0770

The local chapter of the Mechanical Contractors
Association (MCA), established in 1928, represents
management at union-affiliated mechanical contractors. They currently serve 100 member companies, including a number of Gateway contractors.
MCA provides members with education, training,
information services, code assistance, labor relations services, and promotions and public relations.

Medina Supply Co., 230 East Smith Rd.

    Medina, OH, 44258, 216-723-3681

Midland Hardware Co., 1521 West 117th St.

    Cleveland, OH, 44107, 216-228-7721

Miller Cable Co., 210 South Broadway,

    Green Springs, OH, 44836, 419-639-2091

Mohawk Re-Bar Services, 306 Market Ave.

    Canton, OH, 44711, 216-896-6556

Montgomery Elevator Co., 6650 W. Snowville Rd.

    Cleveland, OH, 44141, 216-546-1100

Morabito Trucking, S.B., 3560 East 55th St.

    Cleveland, OH, 44105, 216-441-3070

Museum Services Co., 1220 S.E. Veitch St.

    Gainsville, FL, 32601, 901-338-1800

Myers Appliance, 3280 Kent Rd.

    Stow, OH, 44224, 216-388-0261

N. J. Boupas, Inc., 5550 Sterrett Pl.

    Columbia, MD, 21044, 301-596-4014

Nagel Lyons, 1285 Old River Rd.

    Cleveland, OH, 44113, 216-771-6677

Nagele Mfg. Co., 5201 West 164th St.

    Brookpark, OH, 44142, 216-433-1100

National Precast, Inc., 30066 Little Mack Rd.

    Roseville, MI, 48066, 313-294-6430

Nordonia Building Systems, 8352 Crystal Creek Rd.

    Sagamore Hills, OH, 44067, 216-468-1049

Ohio Diversified Services, Inc., 20643 Avelon Dr.

    Rocky River, OH, 44116, 216-356-7000

Ornamental Iron Works Co., 2900 Newpark Dr.

    Norton, OH, 44203, 216-745-6071

THE OSBORN ENGINEERING CO.

668 Euclid Ave.

Cleveland, OH 44115

216-861-2020

Oster Electric Co., 3907 Perkins Ave.

    Cleveland, OH, 44114, 216-881-1935

Owen Steel Company, 824 Green St.

    Columbia, SC, 29202, 803-251-7680

Ozanne Construction Co., 1635 East 25th St.

    Cleveland, OH, 44114, 216-696-2876

PBC, Inc., 37903 Euclid Ave.

    Willoughby, OH, 44094, 216-975-9494

PMO, Inc., 2225 E. Murray Holladay Rd.

    Salt Lake City, UT, 84117, 801-277-2772

Panzica Construction, 6680 Beta Dr.

    Richmond Hts., OH, 44143, 216-442-4300

Percy Roberts Painting, 918 Hamlin Ave.

    Akron, OH, 44320, 216-376-2199

Peter Hasek Glass Co., 3119 Denison Ave.

    Cleveland, OH, 44109, 216-741-1773

PIPE FITTERS LOCAL UNION NO. 120

6305 Halle Dr., Valley View, OH 44125

216-447-3408

Chartered nearly 95 years ago, Pipe Fitters Local Union No. 120 represents 1,300 active members in the Cleveland area. They provided approximately 100 skilled pipe fitters to more than half a dozen contractors working on Jacobs Field and Gund Arena. Working on the Gateway site for 18 months, union members installed sprinkler, heating and air conditioning, refrigeration and beverage, and arena ice-making systems.

PLUMBERS' UNION, LOCAL NO. 55

1720 East 30th St. Cleveland, OH 44114

216-771-7767

Established more than 100 years ago, Plumbers' Union, Local No. 55 has some 1,200 members, including all of the plumbers who worked on the Gateway facilities. The project had the largest plumbing permit in the history of the City of Cleveland Plumbing Department.

Precision Electric, 595 Golden Oak Pkwy.

Oakwood Village, OH, 44146, 216-439-4414

Proflor, Inc., 8624 Station St.

Mentor, OH, 44060, 216-942-3000

Progressive Brothers, Inc., 12640 Euclid Ave.

Cleveland, OH, 44112, 216-220-6927

Pyramid Electric Co., 33800 Curtis Blvd.

Eastlake, OH, 44095, 216-951-7979

RMC, Inc., 3000 Woodhill Rd.

Cleveland, OH, 44104, 216-229-0500

Raycor Inc., 4500 Lee Rd.

Cleveland, OH, 44128, 216-663-8400

Reliance Mechanical Co., 4975 Hamilton Ave.

Cleveland, OH, 44114, 216-391-1030

RICHARD FLEISCHMAN ARCHITECTS, INC.

1025 Huron Rd., Cleveland, OH 44115

216 771-0090

Richard Fleischman Architects, Inc., founded in 1961, is a multi-faceted design and management firm that provides broad architectural and planning services, including research and programming, program management, feasibility/threshold studies, land-use analysis, facilities evaluation, master planning, and space planning, graphic and interior design. The firm was commissioned to provide architectural and engineering services to construct Gateway's 100,000-square-foot underground service area.

Richard Goettle, Inc., 12071 Hamilton Ave.

Cincinnati, OH, 45231, 513-825-8100

Rittman, Inc./dba Mull Iron, 10 Mull Dr.

Rittman, OH, 44270, 216-927-6855

ROBERT P. MADISON INTERNATIONAL, INC.

2930 Euclid Ave., Cleveland, OH 44115

216-861-8195

Established in 1954, Robert P. Madison International, Inc. (RPMI) was the first minority-owned architectural firm in Ohio and only the 10th in the United States. Now ranked as the eighth largest architectural firm in Northeast Ohio, RPMI maintains three major divisions: urban design and planning, architecture, and engineering. The firm served as the design subcontractor on the Gateway Arena, responsible for producing the architectural working drawings and construction documents.

Robin's Trucking & Storage, 19265 Mumford Rd.

Garrettsville, OH, 44231, 216-548-7711

Rodriguez Distributors, 4245 State Rd.

Cleveland, OH, 44109, 216-398-3400

Romeo Electric Supply, 16912 Miles Ave.

Cleveland, OH, 44128, 216-991-3636

Salerno Construction, 3929 Monticello Blvd.

Cleveland Hts., OH, 44121, 216-291-1486

S.W. FRANKS CONSTRUCTION CO.

2070 West 3rd St., Cleveland, OH 44113

216-664-1600

Samco Inc, 10217 SR 534 North,

Middlefield, OH, 44062, 216-272-5158

SASAKI & ASSOCIATES

64 Pleasant St., Watertown, MA 02172

617-926-3300

Shelter Development Co., 5430 Warner Rd.

Cleveland, OH, 44125, 216-447-9199

Sherwin-Williams Inc, 10740 Broadway Ave.

Cleveland, OH, 44125, 216-271-6766

Shippers Highway Express, 4965 East 154th St.

Cleveland, OH, 44128, 216-475-1411

Sidley Precast, 6900 Madison Rd.

    Thompson, OH, 44086, 216-951-1919

Simon Sign, 6530 Carnegie Ave.

    Cleveland, OH, 44103, 216-361-7753

Singleton Construction Co., 16912 Miles Rd.

    Cleveland, OH, 44128, 216-991-1664

SKYVIEW AERIAL PHOTOGRAPHY, INC.

    20575 CENTER RIDGE ROAD, SUITE 414

    CLEVELAND, OH 44116

    216-356-WIND

Since January 1992, SKYVIEW photography team was at the Gateway site, recording the work in progress from a small, radio-controlled blimp. Breath-taking views of the complex were captured by the ground-based photographer who used a monitor and hand-held remote control to zoom, focus, and adjust the angles of the camera suspended from the 18-foot blimp.

    Morrie Watson and John Markiewicz, who began the company in 1991, have taken thousands of photographs of Gateway at every stage of construction, and are available for sale.

    As Cleveland's renaissance continues, the Skyview blimp will be hovering on the horizon, keeping a vigilant eye on the city's growth. The sky's the limit for both Cleveland and Skyview!

Sony Corporation of America, 7070 Lake Shannon

    Ct., Fenton, MI, 48430, 313-629-6570

Southern Detailing Co., 7280 Pepperoam Ave.

    N. Charleston, SC, 29418, 803-552-7055

Southern Ohio Fabricators, 10333 Wayne Ave.

    Cincinnati, OH, 45215, 513-771-1700

Sterling Painting Co., 3661 Forest Run Dr.

    Richfield, OH, 44286, 216-659-6636

Sussman-Prejza & Co., 3960 Ince Blvd.

    Culver City, CA, 90232, 310-836-3939

T & F Systems, Inc., 1599 East 40th St.

    Cleveland, OH, 44103, 216-881-3525

T. H. Martin Duct Systems, 4545 Commerce Ave.

    Cleveland, OH, 44103, 216-391-0092

Tempglass, Inc., 291 M St.

    Perrysburg, OH, 43551, 419-666-2000

Terra Cotta & Cast Stone, 22001 West 83rd St.

    Shawnee, KS, 66227, 913-422-7575

Thomarios Painting Co., 3636 Summit Rd.

    Norton, OH, 44203, 216-753-5063

Thomas Steel Inc., 305 Elm St.

    Bellevue, OH, 44811, 419-483-7540

Thompson Ground Devel, 8837 St. Clair Ave.

    Cleveland, OH, 44121, 216-851-4333

THOMPSON, HINE & FLORY

    1100 NATIONAL CITY BANK BLDG.

    CLEVELAND, OH 44114

    216-566-5500

Touch Construction, Inc., P.O. Box 6-08128

    Cleveland, OH, 44108, 216-229-5007

Trinity Industries, 1085 Parker St.

    Montgomery, AL, 20000, 205-265-6702

U.S. Fire & Safety Co., 19701 S Miles Road Pkwy.

    Cleveland, OH, 44120, 216-581-1882

Ullman Electric Co., 2299 Glendon Rd.

    Cleveland, OH, 44118, 216-932-3986

Ultrastone-Bellizoni, 4600 Carnegie Ave.

    Cleveland, OH, 44103, 216-391-4412

United Ready-Mix, 1971 Carter Rd.

    Cleveland, OH, 44113, 216-729-0380

Vanderwist & Son, D.R., 4501 Taylor Ln.

    Warrensville Hts., OH, 44128, 216-831-6290

Wagner Sign Co., 7135 West Ridge Rd.

    Elyria, OH, 44035, 216-871-7774

Wayne-Dalton Corp., One Door Dr.

    Mount Hope, OH, 44660, 216-674-7015

Weathermark Corp., 30355 Solon Indust. Pkwy.

    Solon, OH, 44139, 216-498-3800

Weber Company, Inc., 8140 Mayfield Rd.

    Chesterland, OH, 44026, 216-729-0380

Wedding Construction Co., 19249 Calumet Ave.

    Lowell, IN, 46356, 219-696-3050

Western Waterproofing, 13800 Eckles Rd.

    Livonia, MI, 48150, 313-464-3800

Whiteacre Engineering Co., 3833 Progress St., NE

    Canton, OH, 44711, 216-455-8505

Wilkinson Company, 1530 Commerce Dr.

    Stow, OH, 44224, 216-686-9922

Work Best Electric, 924 East Schaaf Rd.

    Brooklyn Hts., OH, 44131, 216-341-1959

Zaranec & Laux, Inc., 5984 Blakley Dr.

    Cleveland, OH, 44143, 215-449-0003

From their offices high in Tower City Center,

the staff of the Gateway Economic Development

Corporation looked down virtually every day

on the ballpark and arena as they were being

built. As the project rose toward completion, the

staff became increasingly emotionally invested

in its success.

As a result, they came to think of themselves not as a staff, but as a team. And as on any good team, there was no unimportant position. From finances to construction coordination to media relations to clerical tasks, Gateway's people took tremendous personal pride in their project. Their dedication and commitment were nonpareil.

Here, then, is the A-team.

Gateway staff, left to right:

W.B. Abshaw,

    Public Relations Assistant

Mary E. Havrilla,

    Information Specialist

John T. Hearns,

    Information Specialist

David G. Hintz,

    Public Relations Assistant

Mark K. Horton,

    Ballpark Project Manager

Susan C. Hunter,

    Special Projects Manager

Luzon Hunnicutt-Thomas,

    Public Relations Manager

PHOTOS OF GATEWAY STAFF: PAUL CHRISTOPHER AND STEVE ZORC

Thanks

For The Memories

The staff of the Gateway Economic Development

Corporation owes a sincere debt of gratitude to a

number of people who helped make our jobs

a little easier during the rough times.

And during the fun times, too.

These people are listed according to the jobs they held when we worked together. Some of them have since moved on to bigger and better things. Wherever they are, we wish them luck.

Cynthia S. Husted,

    Executive Secretary

Edward P. Kovacic,

    Director of Security

Jon W. Kolp,

    Arena Project Manager

John F. Loyd,

    Senior Project Manager

Albert L. Matthews,

    Affirmative Action Compliance

    Manager/Project Manager

Timothy P. Offtermatt,

    Chief Financial Officer

Faith A. Piper,

    Accounting Assistant

Charlestine Randle-Smith,

    Executive Assistant to Executive Director

Not Pictured:

David N. Goss, Vice President, Economic

    Development

Harry C. Howell, VP, Marketing, 1993

Phillip P. Sun, Senior Project Manager, 1991

Gateway: Blueprint Of The Future

Jeff Applebaum of Thompson, Hine, & Flory. Rick Hahn, Steve Nelson, and Bill Roemer of Ameritech. Jim Biggar and Kip Horsburgh of the Gateway board of trustees. Steve Strnisha, finance director of the City of Cleveland. David Abbott, Cuyahoga County Administrator. Tom Henneberry and Terry Keenan of the Richard & David Jacobs Group. Hunter Morrison, Linda Henrichsen, and Ned Reich of the City of Cleveland Department of Planning. Bob Decker, Bob May, Fred Hill, and Joe Tinant of Huber, Hunt & Nichols. Robert DiGeronimo of Independence Excavating. Terry Donley, Jim Nystrand, and Don Dreter of Donley's, Inc. Joanie Schneider, Larry Bignall, and Donna Foxall of Marsh & McLennan. Charles Perry and Wanda Spates of Pinkney Perry Insurance. Nicholas Lessick of Allendale Insurance. Carlton Batson and Ed Lawson of the Bureau of Workers Compensation. Frank Lamb and Nancy Sutter of the Huntington National Bank. Kevin Weigand of Turner Construction. Katie Harrison, Cheryl Jaffe, and Amy Feilen of Rosemont Purchasing. Lee Bartte and Beth deHamel of BT Securities. The Greater Cleveland Growth Association Speakers Bureau. Duane Salls of Bradan Productions, Inc., and Renee McGee for Opening Year festivities.

Gateway would like to thank Cleveland's City Council, including the following:

John E. Barnes, Tyronne Bolden, Dan Brady, Joseph P. Cannon, Roosevelt Coats, George L. Forbes, Gus Frangos, Frank Jackson, Jeffrey D. Johnson, Kenneth L. Johnson, Larry A. Jones, Fannie M. Lewis, Kenneth Lumpkin, David M. McGurik, Dale Miller, Pat O'Malley, William Patmon, Charles L. Patton, Gary Paulenski, Raymond L. Pianka, Michael D. Polensek, Odelia V. Robinson, James Rokakis, Edward W. Rybka, Helen K. Smith, Preston H. Terry, III, Earle B. Turner, Jay Westbrook, Craig E. Willis, Artha Woods.

Robin Sherfield-Bealer,

Receptionist

Lora M. Thompson,

Marketing/Public Relations Director

Kirk R. Wilhelm,

Security Consultant

Toya D. Williams,

Administrative Secretary

Vincent C. Winslow,

Financial Accountant

Alvin Woolen,

Controller/Office Manager

Gateway: Blueprint Of The Future

‘Z a t   R i g h t ?

PHOTO: PAUL CHRISTOPHER ©1994.

League Park

• It might be the most memorable game in
Cleveland history: During the fifth game of the
1920 World Series between Cleveland and
Brooklyn on October 10, Cleveland right fielder
Elmer Smith hit the first grand-slam homer in
World Series history. The ball went over the
right field fence and bounced onto Lexington
Avenue. In the fifth inning of the game,
Cleveland second baseman Bill Wambsganss
turned the first and only unassisted World
Series triple play.

• The youngest Cleveland Indian was Hall of
Fame pitcher "Rapid" Robert Feller, who started with the team in 1936 when he was 17 years
old. The oldest was Phil Niekro, who started in
1987, at the age of 48.

• In 1889, when the players of the newly
formed Cleveland National League team reported to Cleveland, an executive took one look
and exclaimed, "They're skinny and spindly –
just like spiders!" Their white and dark blue
uniforms only served to accentuate the players'
lean appearance, prompting the same official
to observe, "Might as well call them 'Spiders'
and be done with it."

• On July 4, 1911, a team of American League
All-Stars played the Cleveland Indians in a
benefit game for the widow of the late Addie
Joss, who died on April 14 of tubercular
meningitis at the age of 31.

Municipal Stadium

• After a fog-induced delay at Cleveland
Municipal Stadium, Dennis "Oil Can" Boyd, a
Boston Red Sox pitcher who clearly did not
study geography, stated, "That's what happens
when you build a stadium next to the ocean."

• Tribe hurler Leroy "Satchel" Paige was the
first former Negro Leagues pitcher to take the
mound in a World Series, the 1948 contest
between the Indians and the Braves. He was
42 years old and, to his disappointment,
pitched only two-thirds of an inning.

• Cleveland Municipal Stadium is the site of
one of the few forfeited games in modern baseball, when unruly fans took over the field on
the night of June 4, 1974, during a special
promotional event called "Beer Night."

• Only one Indian ever hit four home runs in
one game: Rocky Colavito, against Baltimore
on June 10, 1959.

• The first event held in the still unfinished Municipal Stadium was not a baseball game, but the world's heavyweight title fight. On July 3, 1931, some 40,000 people watched Max Schmeling, the reigning champ, pulverize the contender, William L. "Young" Stribling.

• Earl Averill was the first Indian to hit more than 30 home runs in a season — 32 in 1932. The most recent was Albert Belle — 38 in 1993. The team's single-season home run champ is Al Rosen, who hit 43 in 1953. (Rosen went on to become president of the San Francisco Giants.)

• Only once have Cleveland batters hit four consecutive home runs in one inning: Woodie Held, Pedro Ramos, Tito Francona, and Larry Brown against the Angels on July 31, 1963.

• "Orange Crate": – One of several names that attached themselves to modern baseball gloves in which the thumb and forefinger are joined by deep, wide lacing. Hank Greenberg, general manager of the Cleveland Indians in 1953, may have pioneered the modern "orange crate" or "basket" glove. The same glove was also called the "lobster trap" or "lobster net."

Jacobs Field

• Jacobs Field's $170-million price tag is about 238 times more than what it cost to build the West Side Market in 1913.

• Even though Jacobs Field is only about half the size of Municipal Stadium, it has twice as many restroom stalls as the old stadium. There are also unisex restrooms for disabled and family use.

• Stick around a few years and you'll get to see what's sealed in Gateway's six-foot-long, 100-pound time capsule. Buried in Gateway Plaza and packed with Cleveland memorabilia (including this book), the steel-and-plexiglass capsule will be opened in the year 2064.

• Before construction of the Gateway facility could begin, all existing utilities, including Cleveland Electric Illuminating Company's underground cables, had to be relocated. Relocation of CEI's cables alone cost about $2.5 million.

• The new ballpark, which used 160,000 tons of construction material, cost about $1,050 per ton. Municipal Stadium, which has almost twice as many seats as Jacobs Field, used only 55,000 tons of construction material, and cost about $45 per ton. If the Roman Coliseum (built circa 80 A.D.) were built today with its 800 tons of building material, it would cost about $840 million.

• How much steel does it take to support a ballpark? According to Independence Excavating, about 20,000 tons of structural steel — nearly half a ton for every person who watched the Indians play on Opening Day, 1994 — were used in building Jacobs Field.

• Construction workers found that building a ballpark is a little like putting together an erector set. They had to assemble about 7,500 separate pieces of precast concrete on the site.

• Workers on the ballpark construction site had to yell "Take 'er away!" about 47,500 times while the ballpark was being built. That's how many truckloads of dirt Independence Excavating hauled, amounting to 475,000 cubic yards of dirt — the largest excavation job in Cleveland since the Terminal Tower in 1924. On the most productive day, some 850 loads (or 8500 cubic yards) of dirt were hauled from the ballpark site — a record amount for any project in the city's history.

• Independence Excavating also had to build a temporary earth retention system so that gas lines and other utilities along Carnegie Avenue and Ontario Street wouldn't be disturbed during construction.

• Gateway literally paves the way for Cleveland's future. Its public spaces, designed by Sasaki Associates, Inc., include 5.3 acres of concrete paving and 1.36 miles of new granite curbing, and have more capacity for sound and lighting than any other outdoor location in Cleveland.

• The underground service area (located under the Plaza) took 45,000 tons of concrete — the largest concrete pour in Cleveland history! Built by Donley's, Inc., it is so big it can hold 36 semi tractor-trailers at one time.

• To hold up the new ballpark, Osborn Engineering specified the same 24-inch diameter pipes used in the oil industry.

• Osborn Engineering's structural design for the ballpark, which normally would take about 14 months, was completed in just five months, and included a plan for an underground concourse that allows buses and semi tractor-trailers to be driven completely under the ballpark.

• Jacobs Field's ice production system, designed by Cini·Little, can produce 42 tons of ice for concession stands every 24 hours.

• Cini·Little's refreshment system calls for 625 kegs of beer on tap at any one time (3.9 miles of beer lines), and 7.8 miles of soda lines.

• Jacobs Field seats about 42,500 fans. That's more than twice the student population of Cleveland State University (about 20,000), more than 10 times the number of seats at the Nautica Stage (4,000), and about five and a half times the number of patrons Playhouse Square can accommodate (7,600 seats in the State, Palace and Ohio theaters combined) on any given night. And every seat is bigger than any seat at Municipal Stadium — with more leg room.

• More than 200,000 people work within walking distance of Public Square — and on a summer night, more than 10 percent of them can walk to a baseball game at the new ballpark after work.

• The new ballpark's light towers rise 70 and 80 feet above the top of the stands, beating the average depth of Lake Erie — 65 feet — by just a few feet. The giant scoreboard is even closer to the lake's depth: 67 feet tall.

• Hard Hatted Women set the standard for all other construction projects in the greater Cleveland community, and has set a national record for tradeswomen working on a construction site at one time — 85 women were on the Gateway construction site in August of 1993.

• Gateway was Huber, Hunt & Nichols' 40th completed sports complex.

• S.W. Franks, who installed the playing field at Jacobs Field, also laid 15,000 feet of drainage and irrigation piping, 9,975 tons of drainage material, and 99,000 square feet of sod.

• Miles of electrical wiring, installed by EI-O Electric Company, thread through the complex from top to bottom.

Bats

• Today, Hillerich & Bradsby manufactures more than 1.4 million wood Louisville Slugger bats a year for professional and amateur use. Some bats are still made by hand, as master wood turners use their lathes to shape bats for the boys in the big leagues.

• It takes 40,000 trees to make enough bats for one season.

• Ninety-five percent of all bats are made from Northern White Ash because it has the proper tensile strength, weight, and resiliency required by major league baseball.

• Baseball players are particulary picky about their bats. Ted Williams would go through the wood billets, picking out the ones he wanted. He sent a bat back complaining that the handles weren't right. When it was measured, it *was* off — by 5/1,000th of an inch.

• Harry "The Hat" Walker once saw a bat half-stained, half-unfinished. He liked it, and now the "Walker Finish" is one of seven standard bat styles.

• In the 1970's, George Foster, the National League's leading slugger, used a black-stained

bat that inspired imitations. Reggie Jackson swore there is a night game advantage to black bats: Fielders have a harder time seeing the ball come off the bat.

• Major League baseball stipulates that the longest a bat may be is 42" long, and 2-3/4" wide. Within that specification, a plethora of possibilities exist, with bats weighing no more than 30 ounces to a hefty 37 ounces, with lengths ranging from 30" all the way up to 42".

• The Louisville Slugger took shape from the splinters of Pete "The Old Gladiator" Browning's bat. In 1884, Browning was fighting a slump, and John Andrew "Bud" Hillerich, son of J. Frederich Hillerich, a German immigrant and woodworking shop owner, was watching the game. After the game, the younger Hillerich invited a forlorn Browning to the shop to create a new bat. Browning used the Hillerich bat to go three-for-three the following day, and put the Hillerich family in the bat business. Today, it is the oldest and largest such business in the world.

• The Louisville Slugger was originally known as the "Falls City Slugger."

• On September 1, 1905, "The Flying Dutchman", Honus Wagner, signed a contract giving J.F. Hillerich and Son permission to use his autograph on Louisville Slugger bats. Wagner's signature was the first to be used on a baseball bat, and established the now-widespread practice of endorsement advertising.

• Other greats who signed with H&B and used Louisville Slugger bats to advance their careers include Ty Cobb, Babe Ruth, Ted Williams, Mickey Mantle, Roger Maris, Hank Aaron, Johnny Bench, and George Brett.

Baseballs

• Since 1920, the baseball has undergone only two major changes: In 1926, it went from a cork center to a cushioned cork center; and in 1974 the cover went from horsehide to cowhide. Each major league baseball holds exactly 108 stitches. Each ball is hand-sewn. A good sewer can do six baseballs an hour.

• There are approximately 50,000 dozen (or 600,000) baseballs used each year by major league teams. Each game starts out with about ten dozen; eight for the home team and two dozen for the visiting team.

• What happens to a ball that is thrown out of a game? Baseballs with dings or other irregularities are relegated to the bullpen or batting practice.

• The first Official Baseball Guide, published in 1878, specified that baseballs be supplied by the home club, and shall become the property of the winning club. The Guide also outlined regulations prohibiting doctoring of baseballs: Players found guilty were fined $5.

The seventh inning stretch is not just to relieve stiffening muscles of fans, but was actually intended to bring one's own team luck (the number seven is supposed to be lucky).

Acknowledgements

Gateway Press would like to thank and acknowledge the people who worked on this book and the organizations that supported them.

The core group: Susan M. Tedrick, editor-in-chief and project manager, is a marketing specialist at Grace Communications and American Portrait Films, Cleveland. Edward J. Walsh, author, is the former executive editor of *Corporate Cleveland Magazine*, a Cleveland writer, and editor of Custom Publishing, Inc. Rory O'Connor, editor, is the executive vice president of Whelan Communications Inc., Cleveland. Ben Kotowski, creative director and designer, of Common & Kotowski Graphic Design, Cleveland.

The support group: Mary Mihaly, a Cleveland free-lance writer. Natalie Wester, president, Wester Communications Group, Cleveland.

Photographers: Paul Christopher, a free-lance photographer based in San Mateo, California, for the cover photo of this book, his photos of the finished ballpark and of the people who helped make Jacobs Field a reality.

Jennie Jones, a long-time Cleveland photographer whose work has appeared in a variety of books and magazines. Her studio is at One Cleveland Center on East 9th Street.

Mort Tucker, one of Cleveland's most prominent photographers whose St. Clair Avenue studio in downtown Cleveland is known for its portrait work. Morrie Watson and Jon Markiewicz, Skyview Aerial Photography, who took thousands of Gateway photos from their radio-controlled blimp.

Other support: Computerized Photo Enhancements: The Patrick Joseph Group, Richmond Heights, Ohio. Ned Whelan, Whelan Communications, for his knowledgeable assistance.

Word processing, hard copy scanning, diskette conversions, and taking Susan's messages: Theresa Eble, Whelan Communications.

Proofreading: Sue Sackman.

Design assistance: Steven Gregory, Grace Communications, and Stan Bujak, International Communications.

Marketing, editing and writing assistance: Joan Sanders Palace.

Research assistance: Francine Botti. Larry Lester, Negro Baseball Leagues historian and writer.

General assistance: The staff of the Gateway Economic Development Corporation of Greater Cleveland, notably Luzon Thomas, Lora Thompson, Charlie Randall-Smith, and Tim Offtermatt.

Organizations: The Bettmann Archives, New York, New York. The Cleveland Indians Professional Baseball Club. (Go Tribe!) The Cleveland Museum of Natural History. The Cleveland Public Library. The National Baseball Hall of Fame and Museum, Cooperstown, New York. The Negro Leagues Baseball Museum, Kansas City, Missouri. The Ohio Historical Society, Columbus, Ohio. The Western Reserve Historical Society, Cleveland.

Management and staff of S.P. Mount Printing Co. Cleveland: Mark J. Aliberti, William M. Carran, Jr., Douglas R. Chonko, Jonathan R. Davidson, Clem Davis, Greg Dick, Phil Fulton, Mary Lou Gannon, Al Long, Len Martinson, Gerald L. McGill, Sr., Scott C. McGill, Earl Melvin, Jr., Daniel W. Merritt, Tony Merritt, David Meyers, Harry Moore, Barbara Russo, Roger Spanos, Matthew Sullivan, and Jake Webb.

Other important contributors: Betsy McConahy, Professional Image, Inc., Tulsa, Oklahoma, for printing the cover, dustcovers, and endsheets. Garin Weis, President, Dome Boosters, for research. Rachel Granowicz for specing the book and for paper stock selection. Grace Communications staff for their overall assistance and support during the project: Roy Tidwell, president; Jan Clark, business manager; Kathy Davis; Mary Burich; Marian Mueller; Mark Tichar; Mary Rose Tichar; Christine Tidwell and Tammy Bregitzer.

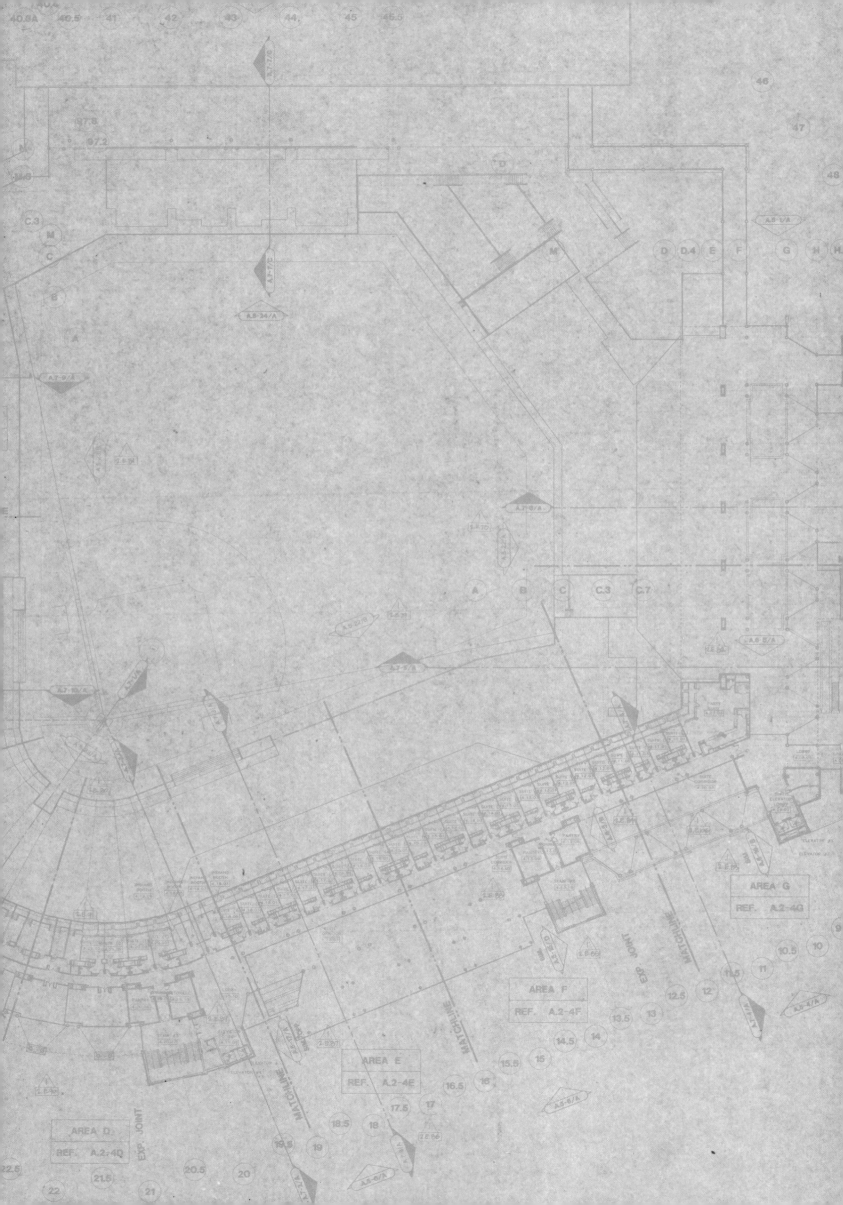